The Examiner

COOKBOOK

**EDITED BY
ROZ CROWLEY**

Published 1995 by C.E.P.L.,
academy street, cork
in association with
on stream publications,
cloghroe, blarney, co. cork.
tel/fax 021 385798

ISBN: 1 897685 90 4

CONTENTS

Unless otherwise stated recipes serve 4

THE AUTHORS

A staff member of Cork Examiner Publications, Phyl Haugh has been writing about cookery for over thirty years. She has been involved in cookery demonstrations for various fund-raising activities and has worked with many of the large food companies testing recipes, adapting them to suit her husband's coeliac diet. She was one of the initiators of the Baking for Giving Competition which plays a large part in providing Christmas cakes and puddings for needy families and individuals in Cork city and county. Her column in the Weekend Examiner continues to be essential weekend reading.

Roz Crowley worked for ten years as RTE Cork's cookery expert and now enjoys meeting producers of food for her Examiner column on Fridays. Her experience as a book editor and researcher began with They've Made It, Ireland's first celebrity cookbook, followed by Kinsale's Good Food Circle Cookbook, The Story of Irish Whiskey and continues with local history and non-fiction publications.

SALADS AND STARTERS

SALADS AND STARTERS

Celebration Cocktail

¼ pint/150 ml French dressing
1 melon, quartered and diced
with seeds removed
1 cucumber, skinned and diced

1 lb/500 g tomatoes, skinned
and diced
2 dessertsp. fresh parsley, finely
chopped

○ Sprinkle the cucumber with some salt and set aside for about 30 minutes to allow excess juices to flow out, then drain it.
○ Combine with the rest of the ingredients and mix well..
○ Allow to chill in the refrigerator or any cool place for a few hours if possible (overnight if you like).
○ Spoon into glasses and serve.   R.C.

Caribbean Curried Chicken Salad

1 lb/450 g shredded cooked
chicken
6 slices pineapple, chopped
1 oz/25 g raisins
1 crisp lettuce
2 tablesp. shredded coconut
2 tablesp. mango chutney

3 oz/75 g peanuts
4 fl oz/125 ml/ ½ cup natural
yoghurt
3 tablesp. mayonnaise
1 teasp. hot curry powder
2 tablesp. chopped parsley

○ Mix the chicken and pineapple together and arrange on top of lettuce in a serving bowl.
○ Pile the raisins, coconut, chutney and peanuts on top.
○ Blend the yoghurt, mayonnaise and curry powder and spoon over the salad. Sprinkle with chopped parsley.
○ Dry roasted peanuts are great in this dish. I sometimes add chopped banana, tossed in lemon juice, instead of the raisins.   P.H.

Lentil Salad

Serves 8-10

This salad keeps well for a few days and is delicious with or on rounds of toasted French bread.

1 lb/480g green or Puy lentils
1 large carrot, diced
1 large onion, diced
1 clove garlic, finely chopped
bouquet garni
pinch white pepper

2⅓ pints/1 ½ litres/2 quarts
water
Dressing:
6 tablesps. olive oil
6 tablesp. wine vinegar

○ Wash and drain lentils, then place in a saucepan with the water and bring to boil.

○ Skim if necessary and add rest of ingredients.

○ Cook, covered, for about 35 minutes or until lentils are cooked but still retaining their shape.

○ Mix the dressing and pour over lentils

○ Mix through and allow to stand for a few hours. The lentils will absorb some of the dressing and become softer.

○ For a special occasion make a paste from a small tin of anchovies liquidized with the oil from the tin and more olive oil to make it spreadable. Spread some anchovy paste on the toasted bread and top with the lentils or place the toasts around lentils heaped on a serving plate.   R.C.

Tangy Potato Salad

1 lb/480 g potatoes, cooked, cooled and cut into chunks
salt
6 fl oz/175 ml/ ¾ US cup mayonnaise
1 tablesp. olive oil

1 tablesp. fresh horseradish, grated, or 2-3 teasp. bottled sauce
freshly ground black pepper
teasp. finely chopped fresh parsley

○ Mix all ingredients and allow to stand for 1 hour. before serving. P.H.

Smoked Mackerel and Cucumber Salad

This is an easy summer salad which is a meal in itself.

2 bunches radishes
1 large cucumber
3 tablesp. olive oil
2 tablesp. lemon juice
2 teasp. wine vinegar

salt & pepper
1 crisp lettuce
4 fillets smoked mackerel
1 lemon, sliced
1 tablesp. chopped chives

○ Slice the radishes and set aside.
○ Peel and chop the cucumber into large dice, sprinkle with salt and leave for 15 minutes.
○ Drain, wash and pat dry with kitchen paper. Mix with the radish.
○ Make the dressing: Place the oil, lemon juice, vinegar and seasoning in a sealed container and shake well.. Pour over the radish and cucumber.
○ Just before serving, arrange the lettuce on a serving dish, top with cucumber and radish mixture and arrange the mackerel fillets on top.
○ Garnish with lemon slices and chopped chives. P.H.

Warm Salads

Salads in winter are all the more attractive if the chill is taken off and some special flavourings added. There are no rules except to use good oil or butter for frying and serve immediately.

○ Fry some small chicken pieces in sesame oil, hazelnut or olive oil and when almost cooked add some lemon juice, a little honey and a teaspoon of grainy mustard to the pan.

○ Toss around until warm and turn out onto a bed of lettuce, juice and all the scrapings form the pan.

○ Do the same with scallops (don't overcook them), kidneys, lamb's liver, chopped bacon and any pieces of game like pigeon breast

○ Cod, cut into small cubes, strips of sole (marinate first in lime or lemon juice), cubes of salmon all make an excellent salad.

○ The main point to remember is to use a good oil for frying and have lemon juice or a good quality vinegar to flavour it, like sherry, raspberry, or-balsamic. All of them should be used sparingly as they have strong flavours. They may seem expensive at first but they go a long way.

○ Buy spinach while it is in season and pick out the younger leaves for a salad. Remove any tough spines and tear the leaves gently. Pour over the warm dressing a few minutes before serving to allow to go limp and lose their toughness (the French call this to 'fatiguer' or tire the leaves). Spinach is particularly good with bacon pieces and croutons fried with garlic.

○ To make the dish more substantial add some chopped hard-boiled egg. Most of the salads will benefit from the addition of toasted nuts like almonds or hazelnuts, or pine nuts for a treat.   R.C.

SALADS AND STARTERS

Hot Black Pudding and Cabbage Salad

Serves 2-4

4 oz/120 g red cabbage
1 tablesp. sesame seeds
1 tablesp. oil (groundnut, olive,
sesame, sunflower)
1 large apple
8 oz/240 g black pudding
4 oz/120 g smoked streaky
bacon, cubed
1 clove garlic, crushed with salt

4 oz/120 g green/white cabbage
Dressing:
2 tsp. grainy mustard
1 tablesp. wine or cider vinegar
or juice half lemon
Salt & black pepper
3 tablesp. oil (sunflower or half
sunflower and olive)

○ Mix dressing together in the order given and set aside.

○ Finely shred the cabbage.

○ In a large frying pan cook the bacon slowly to allow the fat to run, then add the garlic and the red cabbage. Turn up the heat and toss for a minute before adding the green cabbage.

○ When the green cabbage turns bright green it is ready to turn into a warmed bowl

○ Add the sesame seeds and cook until brown, then add into the bowl.

○ Peel and core the apple and slice into thick rounds and cut the black pudding into thick slices.

○ Pour the oil into the pan and add the apple and black pudding. Turn over when crisped a little and cook until the apple begins to soften but still holds its shape.

○ To serve, divide the cabbage between the plates and place the black pudding and apple on top. Pour the dressing into the pan, scrape up any debris and heat through.

○ Pour over the salad and serve immediately.   R.C.

SOUPS

SOUPS

Pea and Cucumber Soup

8 oz/250g frozen peas
1 large potato, sliced
half Spanish onion, sliced
2 pints/1 ¼ litres/1 ¼ quarts
chicken stock (use 3 cubes)
2 oz/50 g butter
1 cucumber, peeled and de
-seeded

2 medium egg yolks
5 fl oz/150 ml/⅔ US cup
5 fl oz/ 150 ml.⅔ US cup thick
cream
salt & black pepper
watercress to garnish

○ Place the peas, potato and a quarter of the stock in a saucepan with half the butter. Simmer for about 20 minutes until the vegetables are tender.

○ Allow to cool slightly.

○ Blend until smooth, adding 4 fl oz/125 ml/½ US cup water.

○ Cut the cucumber into matchsticks and simmer in the remaining butter for 8-10 minutes until tender, turning occasionally to prevent them colouring.

○ Remove from the heat.

○ Beat the egg yolks lightly, add the cream and the purée and beat lightly until well blended.

○ Heat the remaining chicken stock, stir the purée mixture and cook over a low heat, stirring constantly until the soup is smooth and thick. Do not allow to boil.

○ Season to taste, add the cucumber sticks and watercress and serve immediately.   P.H.

Nettle Soup

1 leek or onion
4 oz/120g butter
1 bunch young nettles
1 lb/480g potatoes

2 pints/1¼ litres/1 ¼ quarts
chicken stock
5 fl oz/150ml/⅔ cup cream
salt & pepper

○ Pick the nettles with rubber gloves on and wear the gloves while washing and drying them. They will not lose their sting until cooked. Discard nettle which are large and hairy and late in the season they are past their best for eating.

○ Sweat the leek or inion in the butter for 10 minutes.

○ Add the nettles and cook until glossy.

○ Stir in the potatoes, peeled and sliced, and add the stock.

○ Simmer for 30 minutes or until potatoes are soft.

○ Liquidize and add cream, salt and pepper. Serve hot.

R.C.

Broccoli Cream Soup

Serves 6

1 ½ pints/700 ml chicken stock
1 ¼ lbs/550 g broccoli, sliced
1 stalk celery, thinly sliced
1 small onion, thinly sliced
generous pinch grated nutmeg
salt & black pepper

10 fl oz/275 ml/ 1 ¼ US cups thick cream
Garnish :
lemon slices
salted whipped cream

○ Put the chicken stock in a large pan and bring to the boil. Add the sliced broccoli with the celery and onion.

○ Bring to the boil and simmer for 15-20 minutes or until the vegetables are soft.

○ Purée in a blender or rub through a fine sieve. Season to taste with freshly grated or ground nutmeg, salt and freshly ground black pepper and add the cream until the desired consistency is reached .

○ If the soup is to be served hot, reheat it over a gentle heat without allowing it to boil, stirring continuously. Pour into a heated soup tureen or individual bowls and garnish with slices of lemon and whipped cream seasoned with salt. A tiny inch of nutmeg may be sprinkled over the cream.

○ If serving the soup cold, allow it to cool then chill well in the fridge. Pour into serving bowls and sprinkle with chopped chives or spring onions, a dollop of whipped cream and a tiny pinch of nutmeg.

○ Ground cloves can be substituted for the nutmeg and if you don't want to use cream, cook 1-2 medium potatoes, chopped with the broccoli and use yoghurt to bring the soup to the right consistency.   P.H.

Red Pepper and Tomato Soup
Serves 8-10

4 red peppers
4 small onions
4 cloves garlic
2 potatoes, sliced.
3 oz/90 g butter

2 pints/1¼ litres/1¼ quarts chicken or vegetable stock
8 oz/240 g tinned tomatoes, or fresh, skinned

○ Chop the onions and peppers roughly and garlic cloves into four.

○ Cook gently in the butter in a covered saucepan for 30 minutes or until vegetables are soft.

○ Add the potatoes and stock and simmer for a further 30 minutes.

○ Add the tomatoes, liquidize or sieve and add some black pepper or paprika to taste.

○ The soup at this stage should be smooth and velvety, but add more stock if it is too thick.

○ Serve hot, sprinkled with parsley or tarragon and a blob of cream which looks well on the rich red colour of the soup.

○ In summer this soup may be served chilled. Add chopped chives as garnish.

○ Serve with garlic or herbed bread. R.C.

Leek Soup

2 large leeks, trimmed
4 oz/100 g pickled belly of pork, diced
1 medium onion, grated
1 large potato, diced

¾ pint/450 ml milk
salt & black pepper
4 tablesp. single cream

○ Slice the leeks thinly and rinse well. Drain.

○ Place the pork in a large saucepan and fry gently until the fat runs.

○ Add the onion, leeks and potatoes and stir over moderate heat for 20 minutes. Stir in the milk and season to taste. Bring back to boiling point, cover and simmer for a further 15 minutes, until the pork is tender.

○ Remove from the heat, swirl in the cream and serve hot.   P.H.

SOUPS

Cauliflower Soup

1 cauliflower, broken into florets	'2 pints/1 ¼ litres/1 ¼ quarts chicken stock
2 oz/60 g butter	salt & pepper
1 large onion	1 cup creamy milk
1 large clove garlic	

○ Heat the butter in a heavy saucepan and cook onion and garlic slowly.

○ When soft add the cauliflower sprigs and chopped upstalk and stock.

○ Simmer with the lid on for 1 hour, then cool and sieve, blend or mash.

○ Reheat and add seasoning, then add milk and heat to just below boiling point. Serve scattered with croutons and chopped parsley.　　　R.C.

Tomato and Kidney Soup

1 oz/25 g light margarine	2 pints/1 ¼ litres/1 ¼ quarts beef stock
1 tablesp. sunflower oil	6 oz/175 g dried wholewheat pasta bows or shells
8 oz/250 g lamb's kidneys, skinned, cored and roughly chopped	1 lb/500 g tomatoes, skinned
1 clove garlic, crushed	¼ teasp dried tarragon
1 teasp. tomato paste	2 tablesp. chopped fresh parsley
1 tablesp. plain flour	salt & black pepper
grated rind and juice 2 oranges	

Heat the margarine and oil in a large saucepan and brown the kidneys well. Add the garlic and tomato paste and cook for 1 minute.

Add the flour and cook for 1 minute before adding the stock, orange rind and juice, and the pasta. Bring to the boil, cover and simmer gently for 15-20 minutes or until pasta is cooked.

Halve, seed and roughly chop the tomatoes and stir into the soup with tarragon and parsley. Season and serve hot with crusty French bread.　　P.H.

Cream of Carrot Soup

This is a simple classic soup livened up with dill seed and white wine for a special occasion.

1 oz/30 g butter
4 oz/120g onion, roughly chopped
1 clove garlic, crushed
2 pt/1 ¼ litres/1 ¼ quarts chicken stock
1 oz/30 g rice
½ teasp. dill seeds

3 fl oz/90 ml/⅜ US cup white wine
3 fl oz/90 ml/⅜ US cup cream
seasoning
knob butter
chopped parsley

○ In a large saucepan melt the butter, add the onion and garlic and cook slowly for 5 minutes or until soft.

○ Add the carrots, stock, rice and dill and simmer, covered, for 30 minutes.

○ Add the wine and liquidize.

○ Season to taste and add cream.

○ Add the knob of butter and heat gently without bringing to the boil.

○ Serve sprinkled with chopped parsley.   R.C.

Winter Gold Soup

Serves 8-10

1 lb/450 g Swede turnip	**2 oz/50 g butter**
1 lb/450 g carrots	**1½ pints/900 ml/ 3¾ US cups**
1 lb/450 g parsnips	**stock (use 3 cubes)**
8 oz/225 g potatoes	**salt & pepper to taste**
2 onions	**parsley to garnish**

○ Prepare the vegetables and chop into even-sized pieces.

○ Melt the butter in a saucepan, add all the vegetables and gently cook without browning for 10 minutes.

○ Add the stock, bring to the boil, cover the pan and simmer for 1 hour.

○ Cool slightly then liquidize.

○ Adjust the seasoning and serve hot, with a dollop of cream and chopped parsley.

○ This soup will keep for days and it also freezes very well.

○ The cooking liquid from ham or corned beef makes an excellent stock. Leave the liquid to stand overnight, skim off the fat and use for soup. Cut back on salt when making the soup as the stock will be salty enough. If you think it is salty, add some water to it before making the soup P.H.

Tomato and Corn Soup

This is a quick and easy soup loved by children.

○ Soften **a few sliced onions** (sometimes some sliced garlic) in **butter or oil** (speed the time up by placing a lid on the pan).

○ Add a **tin of tomatoes** (in summer use fresh ones) and a tin or packet of frozen **corn**. and cook for just 10 minutes.

○ Purée or not as desired and serve hot.

○ Grate some cheddar or Parmesan on top just before serving.

○ Basil pesto, that versatile purée of basil and pine nuts, and sometimes Parmesan, is another interesting addition to swirl into finished soups.

○ A treat to serve with this and some of the potato-based soups is hot popcorn over which cheese is finely grated. The light cheese clings to the popcorn and has a real taste of more.

○ Use pasta or noodles to provide substance to soups instead of potatoes.

○ Another idea is to start as usual with butter or oil and some sliced onions, but this time add some sliced cloves of garlic, a chopped rasher or two, a finely sliced carrot and some slivers of celery. When they are soft, add stock and the cooked noodles or pasta.

○ For an even quicker soup just add noodles to stock and float a few chopped spring onions on top.

○ Rashers are also a good addition to the potato and onion based soups.

○ Fresh ginger may be chopped finely with onions and garlic and then any other vegetables before adding stock for a soup with a hint of the Orient.

R.C.

Provencale Fish Chowder

1 ½ lb/750g coley, cod or haddock fillets, skinned and cut into
cubes
3 tablesp. vegetable oil
1 lb/500 g onions, grated
28 oz/850 g can tomatoes
bouquet garni
2 potatoes, cut into cubes
24 black olives, halved and
stoned

2 tablesp. capers, drained
10 fl oz/300 ml/1 ¼ US cups
tomato juice
1 pint/600 ml/2 ½ US cups vegetable stock
salt & black pepper
3 tablesp. chopped parsley

○ Heat the oil in a large saucepan, add the onions and fry gently for 5 minutes until soft and lightly coloured.

○ Add the tomatoes with their juice and the bouquet garni.

○ Bring to the boil, then lower the heat and simmer for 5 minutes, stirring
and breaking up the tomatoes with a wooden spoon.

○ Add the remaining ingredients, except the fish and parsley, and simmer,
uncovered, for 10-15 minutes, or until the potato is cooked.

○ Add the fish and simmer gently, uncovered, for 5 minutes or until tender
but not breaking up.

○ Remove bouquet garni, stir in parsley, taste and adjust seasoning.

○ Transfer to a warmed bowl and serve at once with toasted French bread.

○ Add a crushed clove of garlic for a real Mediterranean flavour.

○ For vegetable stock save the liquid from cooked vegetables such as carrots, potatoes, celery etc. If salt has been used to cook these, bear this in
mind when making the soup and go easy on the seasoning at first. A vegetable stock cube may also be used.

VEGETABLE DISHES

Chilli Vegetable Burgers

4 large potatoes
1 oz/30 g butter
1 cup grated Cheddar cheese
plain flour
breadcrumbs
oil for frying

Filling:
1 carrot
1 courgette, peeled
1 small red pepper
1 small green pepper

1 small onion
1 stick celery
1 oz/30 g butter of oil for frying
1 clove garlic, crushed
1 small fresh red chilli, finely chopped
2 teasp. yellow mustard seeds
2 teasp. coriander seeds
¼ cup water
2 teasp. plain flour
⅔ cup chutney

○ Boil or steam the potatoes until tender; drain mash well with butter, stir in the cheese, cool to room temperature. Shape a tablespoon of potato mixture into a patty shape, top with tablespoon of filling.

○ Place another tablespoon of potato mixture on filling and mould potato around filling to seal completely then shape in to patties. Coat lightly with flour, dip in beaten egg then roll in breadcrumbs.

○ Heat the oil in a frying pan and fry the patties until golden brown.
Filling :

○ Chop all the vegetables finely.

○ Heat the butter or oil in a pan, add the garlic, chilli and spice, cook for 1 minute, stirring.

○ Add vegetables, stir fry for about 5 minutes or until vegetables are soft.

○ Stir in blended water, flour and chutney, stir constantly until mixture boils and thickens.

○ Cool to room temperature before filling the patties.   P.H.

Mushroom and Cheese Soufflé

Serves 4-6

This is an ideal hot starter or supper dish and can be prepared in advance up to the finishing stage. It must be served hot straight from the oven as it will collapse eventually, so have people at the table nibbling at salads or having soup before putting in the oven. It is delicious served with crusty brown or white bread. Do not be daunted by the prospect of making soufflés it's just a whispered rumour that they are difficult.

1 small onion, finely chopped
2 oz/60 g butter
8 oz/240 g mushrooms
salt & pepper
1 heaped teaspoon flour
4 dessertsp. cream
2 rounded dessertsp. butter

1 rounded dessertsp. flour
5 fl oz/150 ml/ ⅔ US cup milk
2 eggs
1 egg white
4 dessertsp. Parmesan cheese
(Cheddar will do)

○ Cook the onion in the 2 oz butter until soft and add the mushrooms.

○ Cook slowly for three minutes and then add the cream and the teaspoon of flour mixed together.

○ Allow to thicken a little and tip into the bottom of a buttered and floured souffle dish or divide between several small ramekin dishes.

○ Sprinkle a little of the cheese around the sides of the dish(es).

○ Preheat the oven to 200C/400F/Gas 6. Melt the rest of the butter in a heavy saucepan and add the flour.

○ Stir well and gradually add the milk, salt and pepper.

○ Separate the yolks from the whites of the eggs and add to the mixture.

○ Add in the cheese.

○ At this stage the mixture can be left until close to serving time.

○ Whisk the 3 egg whites until fairly stiff and fold gently into the mixture, keeping it as light as possible.

○ Turn into the dish and put straight into the hot oven for about 20 minutes (15 minutes for ramekins), or until puffed up and golden.

○ Serve at the table with a crisp green salad.   R.C.

Baked Stuffed Mushrooms

16 large mushrooms
2 oz/60 g butter
1 tablesp. vegetable oil
1 small onion, finely chopped
1 clove garlic, crushed
4 tablesp. fresh white bread-crumbs

1 tablesp. chopped parsley
4 tablesp. grated Parmesan cheese
2 tablesp. single cream
beaten egg
salt & black pepper

○ Preheat the oven to 175C/350F/Gas 4.

○ Remove the stalks from the mushrooms and finely chop the stalk.

○ Melt half the butter and the oil in a frying pan, add the chopped mushroom stalks, onion and crushed garlic and cook until soft but not coloured.

○ Put the breadcrumbs in a bowl with the parsley, cheese and cream.

○ Add just enough beaten egg to bind the mixture together, then stir in the onion and mushroom mixture with salt and pepper to taste.

○ Place the mushrooms, gills uppermost, in an ovenproof dish and divide the stuffing equally between them. Dot with the remaining butter and bake in the preheated oven for 15-20 minutes. Serve hot.

○ Note: If the mushrooms don't have large stalks, use 4 oz/120 g finely chopped button mushrooms.   P.H.

Spinach and Mushroom Lasagna

7 oz/210 g green lasagna (pre-cooked variety)

2 tablesp. vegetable oil

1 onion, finely chopped

4 oz/120 g button mushrooms, sliced

1 lb/480 g green spinach, defrosted and well drained

1-2 tablesp. lemon juice

¼ teasp. grated nutmeg

salt & black pepper

2 oz/60 g cottage cheese

4 oz/120 g Cheddar cheese, grated

butter for seasoning

Sauce:

1 oz/30 g butter

½ oz/15 g plain flour

5 fl oz/150 ml milk

4-5 tablesp. grated Parmesan cheese

○ Heat the oil in a heavy based pan and fry the onion for 3-4 minutes until soft but not coloured.

○ Add the mushrooms and cook, stirring, for 5 minutes. Add the spinach, lemon juice and nutmeg and season with salt and pepper. Simmer for 5-6 minutes, stirring occasionally.

○ Meanwhile, mix the cottage cheese with the grated cheddar in a bowl; season to taste with pepper.

○ Heat the oven to 190C/375F/Gas 5 and grease an 8-inch/20cm square shallow ovenproof dish.

○ **Sauce**: Melt the butter in a small saucepan sprinkle in the flour and stir over a low heat for 1-2 minutes, until straw-coloured. Remove from the heat and gradually stir in the milk. Return to the heat and simmer, stirring, until thick and smooth. Add Parmesan cheese and salt and pepper to taste.

○ Put one-third of the lasagna in the prepared dish, spread with half the cottage cheese mixture, then half the spinach mixture. Repeat the layers. Cover with the remaining lasagna and spread sauce on top.

○ Bake in the pre-heated oven for 30-35 minutes until the top is bubbling and golden.

○ Serve straight from the dish with a tomato and grated carrot salad. P.H.

Potato Curry

1½ teasp. garam masala	1½ lb/720 g potatoes
1½ teasp. ground cumin	¾ cup water
½ teasp. salt	1 cup plain yoghurt
¼ teasp. ground turmeric	1 lb/480 g tin tomatoes, drained
⅛ teasp. cayenne pepper	and chopped
1 tablesp. peeled and minced	1 cup cooked green peas
ginger root	(optional)
2 large garlic cloves, mince	lemon juice
2 cups chopped onion	3 tablesp. corn oil

○ In a bowl combine garam masala, cumin, salt, turmeric and cayenne.

○ In a large heavy frying pan cook the spice mixture, the ginger and the garlic in the oil over moderate heat, stirring, for 1 minute.

○ Add onion and cook, stirring for 10 minutes or until golden. Add potatoes, peeled and cut into 3/4 cubes, and cook, tossing for 2 minutes.

○ Add water and simmer, covered for 5 minutes.

○ Remove lid and increase the heat to moderately high, and add yoghurt. cook, stirring, for 3 minutes or until thickened. Add tomatoes and peas and cook, until heated through.

○ Season with lemon and salt and serve.   R.C.

Mushroom Ketchup

1 lb/480 g mushrooms	¼ teasp. ground ginger
1 oz salt	½ teasp. peppercorns
½ teasp. ground mixed spice	7 fl oz wine vinegar
¼ teasp. ground mace	3 tablesp. brandy (optional)

○ Slice the mushrooms and sprinkle the salt over. Cover and leave overnight.

○ Add all the remaining ingredients except the brandy then liquidize.

○ Simmer for 30 minutes, stir in the brandy and pour into sterilised jars.

○ Cover, cool and store in a cool place. Keeps for at least 3 months. R.C.

Onions Stuffed with Cheese

Serves 10

5 large onions, trimmed and peeled

1 lb ricotta cheese

4 tablesp. chopped parsley

7 oz ham, finely diced

1 egg, beaten

salt and pepper

○ Make one vertical cut from the outside to the centre of each onion. Then put the slit onions in a deep pan of boiling, lightly salted water. Boil for about 15 minutes, until they start to look transparent. The cut will open further. Remove to a bowl of cold water with a slotted spoon to cool.

Stuffing:

○ Mix all remaining ingredients. To separate the onions into layers, slide your thumb beneath each layer in turn and ease it away. When all that remains is a heart about 1" diameter, chop and add to the stuffing.

○ Holding an onion layer in the palm of one hand hollow side uppermost, place a spoonful of stuffing near one side and roll the rest of the layer around it.

○ Thickly butter a large gratin dish. Pack in the onions in a single layer slit side down. Moisten onions with cream and bake in an oven at 175C/350F/Gas 4 oven for about 45 minutes until tender. If necessary, add a little more cream..

○ Left over roast meat or fish may be substituted for the ham..   R.C.

Lemon and Garlic Vegetable Kebabs

1 small corn on the cob, about 5
inches/12.5 cm long
4oz/120g firm tofu, cut into 8
cubes
8 fresh bay leaves
1 courgette, cut into 8 pieces
8 fresh bay leaves
1 courgette, cut into 8 pieces
4 button mushrooms

4 small tomatoes
large clove garlic, crushed
finely grated rind and juice of 1
lemon
4 teasp. olive oil
salt and freshly ground black
pepper
4 oz/120 g long grain rice to
serve

◯ Cook the corn on the cob in plenty of boiling salted water for about 8 minutes. Drain and cut into 8 equal pieces.

◯ Wrap each piece of tofu in a fresh bay leaf. Skewer two pieces on to each of 4 skewers, alternating with the pieces of courgette, mushrooms, tomatoes and corn.

◯ Mix the garlic, lemon rind and juice with the olive oil. Season with salt and pepper.

◯ Lay the kebabs in the mixture, turning to coat well. Cover and refrigerate for at least 30 minutes.   P.H.

Layered Potato Loaf

2 ½ lbs/720 g potatoes
2 oz/60 g clarified butter (made
by melting the butter over low
heat and skimming off the foam
with a paper towel. This avoids
charring and sticking to the tin).

4 oz/120 g cheese, thinly sliced
(Edam style is good, but almost
any type will do, grated fresh
Parmesan is excellent)
fresh thyme
salt & pepper

○ Peel and thinly slice the potatoes. Rinse well to remove some of the starch and dry with a clean teatowel.

○ Coat the slices in the melted butter by tossing around in the saucepan while the butter is still warm.

○ In a well-greased loaf tin, layer the potato slices with the cheese slices, thyme and seasoning.

○ Cover the tin with foil and bake at 425F/220C/Gas 7 for 1 ¼ hours or until the potatoes are tender.

○ Invert the tin onto a serving plate and shake to release the layered potato mould. If the underneath/top isn't brown return it to the oven for 10-20 minutes. Drain off any excess butter and serve immediately.

○ In Switzerland they add a few slices of smoked ham in the layers and use their own Emmenthal or Gruyère cheese to make the same potato dish even richer. It makes an ideal lunch treat with a green salad   R.C.

Sun-Dried Tomatoes

Sun-dried tomatoes are now widely available and are a useful store-cupboard ingredient. If in their dried form, not already re-constituted, they require boiling first in water until they plump up a bit. Then they may be drained, patted dry, and allowed to marinate in olive oil and herbs. I find fresh rosemary good, as are herbes de Provence, especially if they are to sit on slices of toasted French bread later (useful to serve with drinks). They are also good chopped up with olive oil and poured over pasta, on pizzas, on brown bread, in an omelette, and as a base for curries. But why do anything to them? They are delicious eaten in the same way as you might olives, or crisps or peanuts - in your fingers!   R.C.

VEGETABLE DISHES

Sweet and Sour Cabbage

1 red or white cabbage, finely
shredded
2 tablesp. vegetable oil
1 onion, chopped
4 tomatoes, de-seeded and
chopped (optional)

2 tablesp. wine or cider vinegar
1 tablesp. sugar
salt & pepper

○ Heat the oil in a large saucepan and cook the onion until soft
○ Stir in the cabbage, tomatoes, vinegar, salt and pepper..
○ Simmer for 15-20 minutes, depending on desired texture.
○ Add the sugar and cook for a further 2 minutes.
○ Serve immediately.   R.C.

Cabbage in Horseradish Cream Sauce

1½ lb/720 g white cabbage
1 oz/30 g butter
1 oz/30 g plain flour
10 fl oz/300 ml/ 1¼ US cups milk
2 tablesp. horseradish relish

pinch freshly grated nutmeg
freshly ground black pepper
chopped parsley to garnish
salt

○ Discard the tough or discoloured outer leaves and tough inner core.
○ Chop or shred the cabbage finely.
○ Drop cabbage into a pan of salted boiling water and quickly return to
the boil. Continue to boil for 5-7 minutes.
Sauce: Melt the butter in a small saucepan, sprinkle the flour and stir over a
low heat for 2 minutes until straw-coloured, remove from heat and gradually stir in the milk. Return to the heat and simmer, stirring until thick and
smooth. Add the horseradish relish, nutmeg and salt and pepper to taste.
○ Drain the cabbage well, then combine with the sauce. Return to a clean
saucepan, reheat gently then turn into a warmed serving dish. Superb with
steak, roast, or corned beef.and with mackerel.   P.H.

VEGETABLE DISHES

Herby Carrots

1 lb/450 g carrots, cut into
double matchsticks
1 onion, chopped
1 sprig fresh rosemary
1 teasp. chopped parsley

1 clove garlic, crushed
knob butter
salt and pepper
1 tablesp. water
1 tablesp. lightly-whipped cream
(optional)

○ Place all ingredients in a heavy saucepan and cover with a lid.
○ Bring to boil then turn down to cook slowly for about 7 minutes or until the moisture is absorbed and carrots are barely cooked.
○ Serve hot with cream stirred in.   R.C.

Honey and Mustard Turnips

1½ lb/720 g turnips cut into
½ inch/1.25 cm slices
salt
1 oz/30 g butter

2 tablesp. clear honey
2 teasp. soft brown sugar
1 tablesp. French mustard
freshly ground black pepper

○ Heat the oven to 190C/375F/Gas 5.
○ Put the turnips into a saucepan of salted cold water and bring to the boil. Lower the heat and simmer for 5 minutes, then drain the turnips very thoroughly.
○ Meanwhile melt the butter in a small flameproof casserole over a gentle heat. Stir in the honey, sugar, mustard and pepper to taste and let the mixture bubble gently.
○ Tip the turnip slices into the honey mixture, turning them so they are well coated. Cover and cook in the preheated oven for about 45 minutes until tender, stirring occasionally.   P.H.

Lemon Potatoes

Serves 4-6

2 lb/960 g potatoes, peeled	grated rind and juice of 1 lemon
teaspoon butter	2 level tablesp. chopped parsley
1 medium onion, peeled and chopped	salt and pepper

○ Cut potatoes into 1" cubes, put in a large pan, cover with cold water and bring to the boil Simmer for 3 minutes, then drain well.

○ Melt butter in the empty pan, add onion and cook until wilted. Stir in rind and juice, parsley, salt and pepper.

○ Return potatoes to the pan and toss gently so they are evenly coated..Turn into a shallow ovenproof dish. They may be left at this stage in a cool place overnight.

○ Bake in the oven at 190C/375F/Gas 5 for 50 minutes to 1 hour or until golden brown and crisp on top.   R.C.

FISH

Mussels in Garlic Butter

4lbs /2kg mussels, prepared and opened

12 oz/360 g unsalted butter

3-4 cloves of garlic, crushed

finely chopped parsley

O Remove top shell from each mussel and discard. Arrange mussel on half shell in an ovenproof dish.

O Melt the butter in a small saucepan. Add garlic and finely chopped parsley. Pour the hot butter over the mussels.

O Place under a very hot grill or in a very hot oven until sizzling hot.

O Serve with chopped parsley and garnish with lemon wedges. P.H.

Mussels in White Wine

4 lbs/2 kg prepared mussels

1 large onion, finely chopped

½ pint/274 ml dry white wine

2 tablesp. chopped parsley

1 oz/25 g butter

1 oz/25 g flour

salt & black pepper

O Clean the mussels. Put the washed mussels in a large pan with the chopped onion, wine and 1 tablespoon of chopped parsley.

O Cover the pan with a tight fitting lid, bring to the boil and cook over a high heat for about 3-5 minutes, shaking the pan frequently.

O Check if all the mussels are open - they will open when cooked. Discard any that have not opened.

O Strain off the cooking liquid through a layer of muslin or very fine nylon sieve into a small saucepan - keeping the mussels warm by the side of the stove.

O Blend the butter and flour together. Bring the liquid to boil to reduce then whisk in the blended flour and butter mixture in small pieces until the sauce is thickened and smooth. Taste and adjust seasoning then add the remaining parsley.

O Serve the mussels in soup plates. Pour the sauce over them and serve with crusty rolls or French bread.   P.H.

Monkfish or Cod with Rosemary and Garlic
Serves 2

10 oz/300 g monkfish cut into 8 medallions, or 2 cod steaks

2 cloves garlic, finely chopped

1 teaspoon shallots (or onion), finely chopped

clarified butter and olive oil 1 sprig fresh rosemary

flour

salt & white pepper

○ Place equal amounts of butter and oil in a pan and heat. (To clarify the butter heat it and skim the milky solids off the top with a piece of kitchen tissue).

○ Dry the monkfish, season and toss in flour, shaking off any excess.

○ Place the fish in the pan and cook for about 2 minutes each side. Add the rosemary and shallots, cover with foil or a lid and place in the oven for 5 minutes at 350F//180C/Gas 4. A heavy pan may be used on top of the cooker.

○ Remove from the oven, add the garlic and allow to sit for 1 minute in the oven before serving.

○ This is delicious with rice or potatoes and a green salad.   R.C.

Swordfish

Any opportunity of cooking swordfish is well worth taking. Occasionally it arrives in Irish waters and has a fresh light taste despite the denseness of its flesh. It has no small bones and there is little waste from a steak so is excellent value and also freezes well..

○ Lightly coat a frying pan with olive oil

○ Season the fish with black pepper and squeeze over with lemon juice.

○ Fry briskly at first on both sides and then lower the heat and cover with a lid if the steak is thick.

○ Serve with lemon wedges and a green salad. It is delicious cold.

○ Swordfish can also be marinated in olive oil, lemon juice and fresh herbs, and grilled.   R.C.

FISH

Baking Fish 'en Papillote'

Baking fish in greaseproof paper or foil is one of the easiest methods for a party. Individual portions can be prepared early in the day, refrigerated and popped into the oven at the last minute.

For each portion:

◯ Grease a piece of foil or parchment and place any filleted fish on it.

◯ Sprinkle with lemon juice, a little salt and pepper and after that thin strips of vegetables like carrots, mangetout, white turnip, mushrooms, spring onions.

◯ Dot with flakes of butter and fold over the paper or scrunch the foil to make a neat sealed parcel.

◯ A fillet of salmon or thick sole or turbot will take about 20 minutes in a moderate oven. I often use combinations of fish like strips of smoked haddock, sole, turbot, brill together. I use a little minced ginger on fillets of lemon sole for an interesting change.

◯ Separate the different tastes with the vegetables, layering them, keeping a small square shape which looks well when unwrapped. Sometimes I top the parcel off with an unshelled prawn.

◯ Serve the parcels unopened on the plate and supply a bowl for the discarded paper.

◯ All that is needed to finish the dish are some boiled new or baked potatoes and a green salad.   R.C.

Spicey Fried Fish

Serves 2-3

Liven up a dull fillet with some spices for a change. The simplest way is to add some curry powder to the flour with which the fish is coated, but an even better way is this:

1 lb/450 g white fish fillets   **1 teaspoon ground turmeric**
2 tablesp. lemon juice   **½ teaspoon chilli powder**
flour to coat fish   **1 egg beaten**
1 heaped teasp. garam masala   **oil for frying**

○ Squeeze the lemon juice over the fish.
○ Mix the spices and flour together and just before serving coat the fish in the flour, dip into the egg and fry in hot oil for a few minutes.   R.C.

Skate/Ray with Black Butter

This is so simple it hardly needs a recipe. The black butter is more a brown nutty butter which goes well with new potatoes, the ideal accompaniment.

1 lb/480 g ray/skate wing   **3 tablesp. wine vinegar**
1 large onion, sliced   **4 oz unsalted butter**
parsley

○ Wash the fish well in salted water. Place the wing in a wide heavy pan and cover completely with cold water.
○ Add onion and parsley and two spoons of the vinegar.
○ Bring gently to the boil and simmer for 15-20minutes or until the flesh can be separated by pulling with two forks. Turn the fish over halfway during cooking. When ready the fish will be creamy coloured. Place on a hot serving dish.
○ Put the butter in a small saucepan and heat quickly until it foams and begins to turn brown. Pour over the fish. Add the remaining vinegar to the pan, heat and pour over fish. Sprinkle with parsley and serve with potatoes.

R.C.

Poached Scallops with Spring Vegetables
Serves 2 generously

8 oz/240 g small bay scallops (or large scallops quartered)
8 fl oz/250 ml/1 US cup Muscadet or other dry white wine
8 fl oz/250 ml/1 US cup home-made fish stock or court bouil-lon (see next page)

8 fl oz/250 ml double cream or sour cream
salt, pepper
lemon juice
1 carrot, peeled and julienned
1 stalk celery, peeled and juli-enned
julienne = thin matchsticks

○ Clean scallops well and set aside.

○ Combine wine and stock or court bouillon in a saucepan and reduce by half. Strain and discard herbs and vegetables from court bouillon and add scallops to the liquid.

○ Poach gently for about 2 minutes. Remove scallops from liquid, drain and set aside. Add cream to poaching liquid and reduce by half to about 8 fl oz/250 ml. .Season with salt, pepper and drops of lemon juice. Remove from heat.

○ Blanch julienned carrot, celery and courgette very briefly in boiling salt-ed water (or leave raw if desired). Drain and set aside.

○ Return scallops to saucepan with the sauce and heat gently. Place sever-al tablespoons of sauce on each plate. Add scallops in a mound in the cen-tre. top with 1 or 2 tablespoons of sauce. Garnish with the vegetables.R.C.

Family Fish Pie

1 lb/480 g cod	2 tablesp. mayonnaise
8 oz/240 g shelled peas	salt & black pepper
¾ pint 450 ml milk	1½ lbs/720 g potatoes, cooked
1 ½ oz/40 g butter	and mashed
1½oz/40 g flour	
3 hard boiled eggs	

○ Preheat oven to 220C/425F/Gas 7.

○ Skin and wash the cod, put in a pan with the peas and milk. Simmer gently for 10 minutes or until the fish can be flaked with a fork. Tip into a bowl and set aside.

○ Rinse out the pan and then melt the butter. Remove from the heat and stir in the flour, blend well then gradually add the milk strained from the fish.

○ Return the pan to the heat and bring to the boil.

○ Remove any bones from the fish and add to the sauce with the peas, chopped hard boiled eggs, mayonnaise and seasoning. Turn into a 3-pint ovenproof dish.

○ Spread or pipe a border of potatoes around the edge of the dish.

○ Cook in the preheated oven for 30-40 minutes.

○ Garnish with sprigs of parsley and sliced tomato.   P.H.

Court Bouillon

10 fl oz/300 ml/1 ¼ US cups water	1 bay leaf
2 sprigs parsley, chopped	½ teasp. peppercorns
2 shallots, chopped	pinch salt
pinch thyme	½ celery stalk
	½ carrot, chopped

Combine all the ingredients in the pan, cover and bring to the boil. simmer, uncovered, for 20-30 minutes. The finished court bouillon need not necessarily be strained before using.   R.C..

FISH

Smoked Seafood and Pasta Bake

1½ lb/720 g smoked, filleted haddock, cod or coley

3 oz/90 g margarine

2½ oz/75 g plain flour

¾ pint/450 ml milk

½ pint/300 ml fish stock

freshly ground pepper

4 oz/120 g mushrooms, wiped,
trimmed and sliced

6 oz/180 g pasta shells or spirals
cooked

Topping :

4 oz/120 g Edam cheese, grated

sliced tomatoes

○ Preheat oven to 400F/200C/Gas 6.

○ Cut fish into neat pieces then place in a saucepan and cover with cold water. Bring to the boil and simmer for 5-7 minutes.

○ Remove skin and any bones from the fish, discard, then flake the fish and set aside while making the sauce.

Sauce:

○ Melt the margarine in a saucepan over a low heat , stir in the flour to make a roux and cook for 1 minute. Gradually blend in the milk, stirring all the time until the sauce is thickened and smooth, then stir in the fish stock, Taste and adjust the flavour by adding more pepper - remember the fish is salty.

○ Simmer for 5 minutes, stirring frequently.

○ Stir in the flaked fish, sliced mushrooms and cooked pasta, mixing well.

○ Pour into a lightly greased 2 ½-pint fireproof casserole.

○ Sprinkle thickly with grated cheese and arrange sliced tomatoes around the edges of the dish.

○ Cook in the preheated oven for 25-30 minutes until golden and bubbly.

P.H.

CHICKEN

Hot Chilli Pepper Chicken

Hot in more ways than one, the use of fresh hot chillies and large red pepper makes for a lively dish.. Dried chilli powder may be used though the flavour is not as interesting. Be careful when chopping the chillies as they can burn the hands. Wear rubber gloves. Be especially careful not to put chilli-covered hands near your eyes. This recipe comes from the Basque region of southwestern France where unsmoked ham like prosciutto is used. Streaky green bacon is a good substitute.

4 rashers streaky green bacon
oil for frying
4 large chicken pieces
8 cloves garlic, thinly sliced
2 red peppers, thickly sliced

2 hot green chillies, de-seeded and sliced thinly
2 large onions, roughly chopped
2 cans tomatoes

○ Coat a deep frying pan in oil and quickly fry the bacon until just beginning to brown.

○ Add the chicken pieces and brown on all sides. Add the garlic, peppers, chillies and turn down the heat.

○ Sit the chicken pieces on top of the vegetables before placing a tight-fitting lid on top. Cook until tender but check the pan and add a splash of juice from the tomatoes if there is any danger of burning. There should be enough juice from the peppers to allow the chicken to steam.

○ Meanwhile cook the onions in a little oil until tender, then add the tomatoes, breaking them up in the pan, and continue cooking for 20 minutes.

○ To serve place a few spoonfuls of the tomato mixture on a plate with a chicken portion on top and drizzle the remainder on top.   R.C.

Chicken in Cider and Honey

4 chicken portions	2 tablesp. honey
1 oz/30 g polyunsaturated margarine	1 pint/600 ml/2½ US cups dry cider
2 medium onions	1 lb/480 g carrots, sliced
1 oz/30 g wholemeal flour	1 tablesp soy sauce
black pepper	2 tablesp. low fat natural yoghurt

○ Melt the margarine, add the chicken pieces and sauté until golden. Add the sliced onions and cook until soft.

○ Sprinkle the flour over and season. Allow the flour brown slightly then pour in the cider and honey.

○ Add the sliced carrots and soy sauce. Cover, simmer gently for 45-55 minutes, then stir in the yoghurt and check taste for seasoning.

○ Serve with boiled carrots, cauliflower and baked jacket potatoes. P.H

Spicey Citrus Chicken

1 tablesp. plain flour	4 chicken portions, skinned
½ teasp. ground turmeric	1 tablesp. sunflower oil
½ teasp. ground coriander	grated rind and juice 1 orange
½ teasp. ground cumin	grated rind and juice 1 lime
freshly ground black pepper	2 teasp. clear honey

○ Place spices and flour in a bag and add chicken to shake and coat evenly.

○ Heat the oil in a frying pan, add the chicken and cook gently for 5 minutes, turning once.

○ Stir in remaining spiced flour from bag, with orange and lime rinds, juices and honey.

○ Bring to boil and simmer for 15 minutes or until tender. Serve with red lentils,rice, pasta or potatoes   P.H.

CHICKEN

Crispy Spinach Chicken

2 cloves garlic, crushed	¼ pint/150 ml/²/₃ US cup milk
2 oz/60 g smoked streaky bacon	ground black pepper
1 oz/30 g button mushrooms, sliced	6 oz/180 g chicken breasts, skinned
2 oz/60 g cooked spinach	4 oz/120 g butter
1 oz/30 g butter	6 oz/180 g white breadcrumbs
1/2 oz/15 g plain flour	1 tablesp. oil

○ Heat butter and stir in garlic and bacon. Cook for 2-3 minutes, remove with slotted spoon and drain.

○ Stir flour into the butter in the pan and cook for 2 minutes utes. Remove from heat and gradually stir in milk. Stir over medium heat until thickened.

○ Add in bacon, mushrooms and spinach. Season with pepper.

○ Cut chicken breasts horizontally along the side, almost all the way through and spoon the spinach mixture into the pocket.

○ Melt the butter, dip the chicken in it and coat in breadcrumbs. Chill until ready to use.

○ Place on a lightly greased baking sheet and sprinkle with oil. Bake at 190C/375F/Gas 5 for 25 minutes.   P.H.

Chicken Livers with Pasta

Chicken livers are not often found in recipes with pasta but they are delicious and economical. Duck livers are equally good.

○ Fry some chopped **chicken livers** with a chopped **onion** and a clove of **garlic** in a little **butter.** until onion is soft but livers not dried out. Add a splash of **cream** and some tinned **butter beans.** Season with black pepper and serve with any pasta shape, tagliatelle is probably best..   R.C.

Poulet Vallée d'Auge

Chicken cooked with apples is a mouthwatering idea from Normandy in France, home of the superb Calvados brandy. The chicken is usually cooked whole but this version is easier.

2 streaky rashers, chopped
1 large onion, chopped finely
1 stalk celery, chopped finely
knob butter
4 large chicken joints
2 large cooking apples, peeled and cut into chunks
splash Calvados (optional)

1 mug (10 fl oz) cider or apple juice
2 sage leaves or sprig thyme or dried equivalents
salt & black pepper.
cream (optional)
1 egg yolk
(optional)

○ Brown the rasher pieces in the butter in a deep frying pan, add the onions and celery toss around and turn the heat down.

○ Allow to cook until soft then turn the heat up and brown the chicken pieces on all sides. At this point the French would add the Calvados and set it alight in the pan.

○ Add the apples, toss around, and then add liquid. The cider or apple juice should come half way up the chicken joints.

○ Add the herb and season with salt & black pepper.

○ Cover and cook for about 20 minutes or until the joints are cooked through. This can also be done in a casserole in a moderate oven.

○ Remove the joints and apple pieces from the pan and keep warm while the liquid is boiled down to a thick syrupy consistency.

○ At this stage the French add the cream mixed with an egg yolk and reduce the liquid further to get a thick creamy texture. I prefer to mash one or two of the apple chunks into the sauce.

○ Serve with potatoes or rice and a green salad.   R.C.

PORK AND HAM

Loin of Pork with Piquant Sauce

1 loin of pork weighing approx.
3 lbs/1 ½ kgs
glaze:
8 oz/225 g can pineapple pieces
½ pint/275 ml water
2 oz/60 g/1 ¼ US cups golden
syrup
1 level teasp. dry mustard

1 level teasp. salt
½ level teasp. salt
¼ level teasp. freshly ground
black pepper
½ oz/15 g cornflour
1 chicken stock cube
1 tablesp. redcurrant jelly
1 tablesp. vinegar

Oven temperature: 375F/190C/Gas 5

○ Place the meat in a roasting tin or casserole.

○ Drain the pineapple and mix the juice with ½ pint/275 ml water..

○ Blend the golden syrup, mustard, salt and pepper with the fruit juice and water. Pour over the meat, cover with foil or lid and cook, basting every 30 minutes or so, allowing 30 minutes before the end of cooking time.

○ Transfer meat to a heated serving dish.

○ Mix the cornflour in a little cold water. Blend it, together with the crushed stock cube, redcurrant jelly and vinegar with the liquid from the roasting tin.

○ Bring to the boil on top of the cooker, stirring all the time.

○ Chop up the pineapple and add to the sauce. adjust the seasoning if necessary.

○ Serve with cauliflower florets and carrots tossed in melted butter.

P.H.

PORK AND HAM

Stir-Fry Pork with Chilli

1 lb/480 g lean pork, cut into strips

cooking oil

1 bunch scallions, trimmed and cut into matchsticks

2 large yellow peppers, deseeded and cut into strips

Marinade:

2 cloves garlic, chopped

1 fresh chilli, cut into thin circles

1 tablesp. oil

1 tablesp. dry sherry

1 tablesp. light soy sauce

1 teasp. caster sugar

1 teasp. cornflour

○ Blend marinade ingredients and pour over pork strips to marinate for a few hours or until required.

○ Heat a little oil in a wok or large frying pan and fry scallions and peppers for 2-3 minutes. Remove from pan.

○ Add pork in batches and fry for 3 minutes, stirring briskly. Return vegetables to pan and heat through.

○ Serve with noodles.   P.H.

Pork Sausages with Pasta

○ Slowly fry a **chopped onion, garlic and a carrot in olive oil** for ten minutes.

○ Add a **can of tomatoes** or some skinned fresh tomatoes.(The jars of bolognese sauces now available are a good substitute).

○ Cut up the sausages (which can also be beef or lamb) into bite sizes and cook them slowly in the sauce.One per person is usually enough.

○ Sprinkle with **fresh basil or tarragon** when available and for a more substantial meal some **Parmesan cheese**. Other cheeses, even blue styles are also delicious.

○ Italians will tell you that pasta should be served 'al dente', firm to the teeth, and not soft and flabby. To make sure of this the water should be fast-boiling and have a handful of salt added. Use a large saucepan so the pasta can move freely.   R.C.

Italian Pork Casserole

3 tablesp. polyunsaturated oil
2 lb/1 kg pork fillet, trimmed
and diced
freshly ground black pepper
2 cloves garlic, skinned and
chopped

8 oz/240 g tomatoes, skinned
and chopped
½ pint/300 ml/1 ¼ US cups
orange juice/4 tablesp./20 ml
tomato purée
2 sprigs of rosemary
strip of lemon rind

○ Heat the oil in a frying pan. Add the meat, season with black pepper and cook until the meat is golden brown, about 8-10 minutes.

○ Add the garlic. Stir in the orange juice, tomatoes, tomato purée, rosemary and lemon rind and add just enough water to cover.

○ Pour into a casserole, cover with tightly fitting lid and cook in the centre of the oven at 180C/350F/Gas Mark 4 for about 1 hour or until the meat is tender.

○ Remove the rosemary and lemon rind before serving.

○ Serve with wholegrain rice and a selection of salads. P.H.

Pork Steaks

Useful for quick stir frying, another quick way to cook pork steaks is to use them like veal escalopes.

○ Divide the steak into four and flatten each piece with a rolling pin. (Place each piece in a supermarket bag to prevent the meat from sticking to the rolling pin).

○ Dust each piece with seasoned flour, dip into egg, then herbed breadcrumbs and fry on both sides until cooked through.

○ Serve with a wedge of lemon, creamy mashed potatoes, and a green salad. R.C.

PORK AND HAM

Pork Chops in Cider Sauce

4 medium pork chops
3 tablesp. plain flour
salt & black pepper
pinch ground mace (optional)
2 oz/60 g butter
8 spring onions, thinly sliced

¼ pint/150 ml/⅔ US cup dry cider
1 teasp. tomato purée
4 thin slices lemon
1 tablesp. cream (optional)

○ Trim meat, discarding any rind or fat. Put flour into a bag, season with salt & pepper and mace. Toss chops in the flour until coated.

○ Melt butter in a large frying pan over moderate heat and when it stops foaming add the chops. Fry gently for about 8 minutes.

○ Turn each chop carefully taking care not to pierce the meat and fry for a further 5 minutes until cooked through and browned.

○ Transfer to a warmed serving dish, cover with foil and keep warm in a low oven.

○ Add the 8 onions to the fat in the pan and cook for 3 minutes. Add cider, tomato purée and bring to the boil. Add the lemon slices and boil for 1 minute.

○ Taste the sauce and season with salt and pepper and stir in cream or milk if the sauce is too sharp.

○ Pour the sauce over the chops and heat through for 5 minutes.

○ Serve with buttered pasta shells, rice or boiled potatoes, and sprouts or green beans.   P.H.

Leeks in Ham

○ Boil some washed and trimmed **leeks** in water for 5-10 minutes, depending on size.

○ Drain and wrap in a slice of **ham** individually. Place in a casserole dish and cover with **white sauce** (butter, flour and milk or milk and stock, and a little mixed herbs for extra flavour). Sprinkle with grated **cheese** and bake at 175C/350F/Gas 4, for 30minutes, or place in microwave for a few minutes on high until hot. Excellent with garlic bread.   R.C.

Ham and Cheese Pudding

2 slices bread, cut into triangles
½ oz/15 g butter or margarine
1 small onion, finely chopped
1 or 2 slices cooked ham, chopped
2 oz/60 g Cheddar cheese, grated
1 egg

¼ pint/150 ml milk
salt & pepper
1 large tomato, sliced
2 teasp. chopped fresh or 1 teasp. dried chives
1-2 teasp. vinegar

○ Preheat oven to 190C/375F/Gas 5.

○ Place half the bread in an individual ovenproof dish.

○ Melt the butter and add most of the onion, stir-frying for about 2 minutes until softened. Sprinkle on the bread and add the ham and half the cheese.

○ Cover with the remaining bread.

○ Beat together the egg and milk, season with salt & pepper and pour carefully over the bread. Leave to soak for 5 minutes, then sprinkle the remaining cheese on top.

○ Bake in the oven for 20-25 minutes or until puffed up and golden. P.H.

PORK AND HAM

Cider Bacon Bake

3 ½ lb/1.6 kg unsmoked collar
bacon, soaked overnight
8 whole cloves
finely grated rind and juice
1 large orange
1 tablesp. clear honey
2 tablesp. dark soft brown sugar
15 fl oz/450 ml dry cider

2 cooking apples, peeled and
sliced

To glaze and garnish:
wholes cloves to decorate
2 tablesp. golden syrup
2 tablesp. demerara sugar

○ Drain the bacon and rinse well under cold running water.

○ Stud the skin with cloves, then place the joint in a large casserole.

○ Mix together the orange rind and juice, honey, sugar and then stir in the cider gradually.

○ Pour over the bacon then add the apple slices.

○ Cover and cook in a slow oven 225F/110C/Gas ¼ for at least 8 hours until the bacon is tender.

○ Remove the casserole from the oven and increase the heat to 230C/450F/Gas 8.

○ Remove the bacon from the casserole and deep the remaining cooking liquid hot. Slice off and discard the skin from the bacon, leaving a thin layer of fat. Stand the joint on a rack in a roasting tin.

○ To glaze: Score the fat into diamond shapes with a sharp knife. stud the diamonds with whole cloves then spread with the syrup and sprinkle with the demerara sugar. Bake for about 20 minutes until golden.   P.H.

Baked Glazed Corned Beef

Corned Beef is an economical dish and this recipe makes it special.

1 large piece corned silverside
1 level tablesp. mixed spice
1 large stalk of celery
1 onion, chopped
1 carrot, chopped

few whole cloves
3 tablesp. honey
1 level tablesp. prepared mustard
3 tablesp. orange juice
2 tablesp. water

○ Rinse the beef under cold running water and place in a large saucepan. Cover with cold water.

○ Add spices, celery, onion and carrot. Bring to the boil, cover and simmer gently for about 3 hours, depending on weight (allow 25 mins per lb or until the meat is tender.)

○ Allow to cool in the broth (which is ideal for soup). Drain the beef and place it in a shallow baking dish. Score the layer of fat and stud with cloves.

○ Pour the orange juice over the meat, mix the honey and mustard and pat it over the top of the beef.

○ Pour the water into the baking dish then cook the meat for about 45 minutes at 180C/350F/Gas 4, basting frequently with the juices in the pan.

○ Pat a little extra honey onto the meat after half an hour.

○ Serve hot with vegetable or cold with salad   P.H.

Tripe and Onions

Tripe is a traditional Cork dish and here the best of its flavour is brought out with the addition of onions and seasoning.

1½ lb/720 g tripe

1½ lb Spanish onions, peeled and left whole

2/3 sticks celery

salt

6-8 whole black peppercorns

few sprigs parsley

1 oz/30 g butter

1 oz/30 g plain flour

½ pint/300 g/1¼ US cups milk

pinch freshly grated nutmeg

freshly ground black pepper

2 tablesp. capers, drained

1 tablesp. chopped fresh parsley

4 slices white bread crusts removed

○ Put the tripe in a large saucepan, cover with cold water and bring to the boil. Drain off the water.

○ Add the whole onion, celery salt, peppercorns and parsley to the tripe in the pan, cover with fresh cold water and bring to the boil again.

○ Lower the heat, cover the pan and simmer for 1½ hours or until the tripe is tender when pierced with the point of a sharp knife.

○ Strain off the cooking liquid and reserve ½ pint of it for the sauce. Leave the tripe until cool enough to handle then cut it into ½ inch squares and thickly slice the cooked onions.

○ Melt the butter in a large saucepan, sprinkle in the flour and stir over low heat for 1-2 minutes until straw-coloured. Remove from the heat and gradually stir in the reserved cooking liquid, followed by the milk. Return to the heat and simmer, stirring , until, thick and smooth. Add the nutmeg, salt and pepper to taste, then the tripe, onion and capers. Simmer for a further 20 minutes.

○ Just before the end for the cooking time, toast the bread on both sides and cut each slice into triangles.

○ Turn the tripe and sauce into a warmed serving dish, sprinkle with parsley and arrange the toast triangles around the edge of the dish.

○ Serve at once while piping hot, with fluffy mashed potatoes.

○ Crispy grilled streaky rashers are delicious on top of the tripe. Capers can be left out if you don't fancy them - the dish will taste delicious.   P.H.

BEEF

Pressed Ox Tongue

Ox tongues are inexpensive these days as no-one seems to want to cook them. They are easier to cook and tastier than most people realise, and are excellent sliced thinly for sandwiches.

1 pickled ox tongue	**6 peppercorns**
1 large onion, chopped	**1 bayleaf**
2 carrots, chopped	**2 teasp. gelatine powder**
2 sticks celery, chopped	**2 tablesp. port**
A few sprigs parsley	

○ Scrub the tongue well, then soak it for a couple of hours in cold water..

○ Place the tongue in a fresh pot of cold water and bring to the boil. Skim away all surface scum before adding the vegetables, parsley, peppercorns, and bayleaf..

○ Simmer very gently for about 3 hours.

○ Remove the tongue from the saucepan, hold it under the running cold tap and strip away all the skin. Trim the ragged and gristly bits of meat at the root, then curl the tongue around and fit into a tin or dish or saucepan.

○ Boil the cooking liquid briskly and reduce it to concentrate the flavour.

○ Sprinkle the gelatine onto about 2 tablespoons of cold water in a cup, dissolve it over simmering water until absolutely clear before stirring it into 1½ pint/300 ml of the cooking liquid.

○ Add the port and pour the mixture over the tongue. Put a saucer on top, weight it heavily, then leave until cold and set.

○ Slice and serve with salad and Cumberland Sauce (recipe next page).

○ Tongue can also be served with first being pressed. When it is cooked, remove the skin and any gristly bits and just allow it to cool..   P.H.

Tongue Paté

1 lb cooked tongue	salt
Pinch each of	black pepper
powdered mace	3 tbls/45 ml/⅛ US cup red wine
mixed spice	or Dry Martini
cayenne pepper	8 oz/240 g butter

○ Shred the tongue finely, or liquidize, then mix in red wine.

○ Add spices and three quarters of the butter and mix until smooth.

○ Check for seasoning and pack into small pots for use separately, or in a terrine or loaf tin.

○ Melt the remaining butter until foaming and pour over the tops of the pots to seal. Place a bayleaf on top for decoration.

○ Cool, then refrigerate until ready to serve.

○ Allow to come to room temperature before slicing and serving with Cumberland sauce or any tart or sweet relish.

○ This recipe may also be used for left over ham, chicken, turkey and salmon. Go easy on the spices when using fish.   R.C.

Cumberland Sauce

1 orange	4 tablesp. port
1 lemon	1 teasp. dried mustard powder
4 large tablesp. redcurrant jelly	1 teasp. ground ginger

○ Pare the rinds of both the lemon and orange. Cut into tiny, thin strip. Boil the rinds in water for 5-6 minutes to extract any bitterness and then drain well in a sieve.

○ Place the redcurrant jelly in a small saucepan with the port and melt them together over a low heat for about 5 minutes.

○ Mix the mustard and ginger with the juice of half a lemon until smooth. Add to the pan.

○ Add the juice of the whole orange and finally the little strips of orange and lemon peel. Mix well, cool in the fridge before serving.

○ Serve cold and keep in a screw top jar in the fridge.   P.H.

BEEF

Battered Beef Bake

500 g/1 lb blade steak cut into 1½ inch cubes
1 oz/25 g dripping or cooking oil
Batter:
6 oz /175 g plain flour
½ teasp. salt
2 eggs
¾ pint /425 ml /1 ¾ US cups milk and water mixture
¼ teasp. dried mixed herbs
freshly ground pepper

○ Preheat the oven to 220C/425F/Gas 7.

○ Make the batter: sift the flour and salt into a large bowl and make a well in the centre. Beat the eggs with the milk and water mixture and pour into the well gradually drawing the flour into the liquid with a wooden spoon.

○ When all the liquid is incorporated add the herbs and pepper to taste. Beat well to make a smooth batter, then set aside while browning the beef.

○ Melt the dripping or oil in a frying pan and when just sizzling add the beef cubes. Cook briskly for 5-10 minutes turning from time to time until they are sealed and browned on all sides.

○ Remove the beef cubes with a slotted spoon. Drain off the fat and juices remaining in the pan into a warmed roasting tin.

○ Swirl the fat around the sides of the dish and then arrange the beef cubes in it in a single layer.

○ Immediately pour the batter over the beef and bake in the preheated oven for 40-50 minutes until well risen, golden brown and crisp at the edges.

○ Serve at once, cut into squares, straight from the dish.

○ Carrots, spinach or broccoli go very well with this dish.

○ I sometimes fry some onion rings when the beef has been browned and put them into the roasting tin before adding the beef.. You might need to add extra fat to the pan. Mushrooms too could be used.   P.H.

Beef and Mushroom Pie

Makes 2 pies to serve 4-6 each

2 ½ lbs/1.2 kg blade steak in the piece
3 oz/90 g seasoned flour
2 onions, sliced
¼ pint/150 ml/⅔ US cup stout

¼ pint/150 ml/⅔ US cup sherry
1 ½ pints/900 ml/3 ¾ US cups beef stock
4 oz/120 g button mushrooms
4 tablesp. mushroom ketchup

○ Place the sliced onions in a shallow oven-proof dish.

○ Lay the meat on top and rub as much flour into it as possible, sprinkle the remaining flour on top.

○ Bring all the liquids to the boil and pour onto the meat.

○ Cover with a lid or foil and cook in the oven for 3 hours at 275F/140C/Gas 1. The heat should be so low that the meat barely simmers.

○ When the meat is tender which it should be after 3 hours (if not add some more liquid and cook it further), with two forks pull the meat apart into bite-sized chunks.

○ Stir in the mushrooms and ketchup. At this stage the dish can be allowed to cool and then be kept overnight in a cool place.

○ To finish the pies:

○ About 45 minutes before serving, put the cooked filling into the dishes lined with pastry. Arrange pastry leaves, made from scraps of leftover pastry, over the top and brush with milk or an egg and milk glaze.

○ Bake at 375F/190C/Gas 5 for 35-40 minutes or until the pastry is well browned. The pastry won't suffer from being under the meat if you don't fill the pies too long before cooking and it's better not to use pie dishes which are very heavy as you want the heat to get at the pastry.

To make the pastry:

○ Mix together 1 lb/480 g plain flour, ½ teaspoon salt, 12 oz/360 g butter, and enough water to make a sticky dough. Work the ingredients together until the dough has lost its stickiness and is smooth. Wrap in clingfilm and chill until firm.

See page 26 for recipe for mushroom ketchup   R. C.

Polpette

In Italy these burgers are traditionally made with veal, but beef, pork or lamb mince is excellent. If using fatty meat grill it slowly or sit on a dry pan on low heat to allow the fat to drip off before starting the recipe.

1 lb mince
4 oz/120 g Parmesan or Regato cheese
large handful breadcrumbs
2 dessertsp. chopped parsley

1 egg
breadcrumbs for coating
1 grated apple sprinkled with lemon juice if using pork mince
oil for frying

○ Stir all ingredients except the coating crumbs until evenly mixed (reserve a little cheese for sprinkling before serving).

○ Form into balls the size of a 5p and flatten.

○ Coat with breadcrumbs.

○ They may be kept in the 'fridge for a day or two at this stage.

○ Heat the oil and fry a little garlic to flavour the oil and remove before adding the burgers a few at a time. They will not require much cooking as they are so small.

○ Sprinkle with cheese and serve with a tomato salad made by sprinkling olive oil and salt over sliced tomatoes.

○ New potatoes are particularly good with this dish as are creamy mashed potatoes.   R.C.

LAMB

LAMB

Roast Lamb with Garlic

Lamb is unthinkable without garlic. Some garlic lovers like to place slivers of peeled garlic close to the bone and through the flesh. Here it is roasted, unpeeled, with the joint to serve to those who really love it.

leg of lamb, trimmed	**2 large sprigs rosemary**
1 tablesp. olive oil	**2 slices lemon**
2 bulbs garlic	**salt & black pepper**

○ Preheat oven to 180C/350F/Gas 4.

○ Heat the oil in a heavy casserole dish which has a tightly fitting lid and brown the lamb all over.

○ Break up the garlic bulbs into cloves and place around the joint with the rosemary and lemon. Season with salt & pepper.

○ Cover the dish tightly with tinfoil and its lid. Cook for 2 -2 ½ hours.

○ When cooked wrap in foil to rest before serving.

○ Boil up the juices in the casserole dish and serve over the lamb with the unpeeled cloves ready to be squeezed out.   P.H.

○ In France, particularly in Normandy, lamb is roasted as in Phyl's recipe above and then served with haricot beans, onions, garlic and tomatoes. If you have the patience to soak and boil haricot beans for hours, the recipe will be more authentic, but canned butter beans are a good lazy alternative.

○ Fry the onions, garlic and a chopped carrot in a little oil until soft, then add a few tomatoes (canned or fresh) and a little thyme and simmer gently to a pulp.

○ Add the butter beans and heat them through and the vegetable dish is ready to eat at any time.

○ Leftovers are delicious with bread.   R.C.

LAMB

Lamb with Salted Lemon
Serves 4-6

6 tablesp. olive oil
1 clove garlic, crushed
1 small piece fresh ginger, crushed
¼ teasp. powdered saffron
2 lbs/1 kg boneless lamb, leg or

neck fillet, cubed
2 Spanish onions, finely chopped
1 salted lemon
2 lbs/1 kg scraped new potatoes
salt and freshly-ground pepper

○ Put the oil, crushed garlic, ginger and saffron into a big, wide pan. Add the lamb and turn to coat it with the oil. Add the onions.
○ Divide the lemon into quarters, remove and discard the flesh and pith, and add the skin to the pan with enough water to cover the lamb. Bring to the boil, lower the heat and simmer until the lamb is almost tender. this may take up to two hours.
○ Add the potatoes and continue cooking until the potatoes are tender. If there is still too much liquid, take out the meat and vegetables and keep warm, whilst reducing the sauce by fast boiling. Season with salt, if needed and freshly-ground black pepper.
○ This dish can be cooked in advance and reheated. It can also be frozen.
○ Hot French bread and a mixed green salad complete this easy meal.

R. C.

Salted Lemons
7 firm, thin-skinned lemons   7 tablesp. sea salt

○ Scrub the lemons with warm water and a soft brush, and scald a pre-serving jar which is large enough to hold all the fruit.
○ Using a stainless-steel knife, cut six of the lemons lengthwise as if into quarters, but not right through. Pack a tablespoonful of salt into each one and pack them tightly into the jar. Add the remaining salt and juice of the seventh lemon. Top up with boiling water to cover the fruit. Close the jar tightly and leave it for two or three weeks in a cool, dark place. Once matured, salted lemons keep well for many months.   R. C.

Lamb with Cumin

This recipe has spices of the Orient at their mysterious and complex best with the flavour of cumin predominating.

1 tablesp. whole cumin seeds	1 teasp. salt
2 inch/5 cm piece fresh ginger, peeled and chopped	2 teasp. brown sugar
	6 fl oz/175 ml/¾ US cup yoghurt
4 garlic cloves	2 oz/60 g butter
2 teasp. cardamom seeds	1 large onion, finely chopped
2 whole cloves	2 lb/1 kg lamb pieces
3 teasp. sesame seeds	pinch/1 long thread saffron
4 oz/120 g blanched almonds	(optional)
1 teasp. cayenne pepper	

○ Place the cumin, ginger, garlic, cardamom, cloves, almonds, sesame, cayenne, sugar, salt and one third of the yoghurt into a blender to make a paste.

○ Melt the butter in a wide pan and fry the onion gently until golden. Stir in the spice paste and fry for 5 minutes, stirring constantly to bring out the flavours.

○ Add the lamb and brown all over.

○ Mix together the yoghurt and saffron (not essential), add to the pan and bring to the boil.

○ Lower the heat and simmer for 1 ½ hours or place in a casserole dish and cook in the oven at 160C/325F/Gas 3 for 2 hours or until meat is tender.

○ Serve with Basmati or brown rice and a crisp green salad.   R.C.

LAMB

Spicey Lamb with Prunes

Prunes are delicious with lamb and this is an easy recipe combining both.

1½ lb/720 g lean lamb pieces
2 tablesp. vegetable oil
1 onion, chopped
½ teasp. ground ginger
¼ teasp. ground cinnamon

1 pint/20 fl oz/600 ml/2½ US cups chicken stock
4 oz/120 g prunes, soaked in boiling water
2 tart eating apples
1 tablesp. clear honey

○ Heat the oil in a large flameproof casserole, add the onion and fry over moderate heat for 2 minutes.

○ Add the lamb, increase the heat and fry until browned.

○ Sprinkle on the ginger and cinnamon, stir in the stock and bring to boil.

○ Lower the heat, cover the pan and simmer gently for 1 ½ hours, until the meat is tender.

○ Drain the prunes and remove the stones.

○ Peel, core and quarter the apples and slice thickly. Add to the pan with the prunes and honey.

○ Stir well and simmer for 20 minutes until the apples and prunes have softened.

○ Delicious with rice or couscous.   P.H.

LAMB

Lamb Casserole with Courgette and Lemon

When courgettes are out of season substitute with cauliflower or green beans. Tinned tomatoes can be used.

1 shoulder lamb, boned, trimmed and cut into 1 inch cubes
oil for frying
1 onion, finely chopped
3 cloves garlic, chopped
1 tablesp. wholemeal flour
¾ pint/375 ml/1½ cups water or
stock
1 lb/480 g tomatoes, chopped
juice and rind 1 large lemon
3 tablesp. fresh oregano or marjoram, chopped or 1 teasp.dried
salt & pepper
1 lb/480 g courgettes, chopped.

○ Preheat oven to 180C/350F/Gas 4.
○ Heat oil and brown lamb a little at a time.
○ Remove meat from casserole and add onions. Cook for a few minutes then stir in the flour and garlic and cook for a further 2 minutes.
○ Add the stock or water, half the tomatoes, lemon juice, rind and herbs and mix well.
○ Bring to the boil and cook for a few minutes.
○ Add the meat back into the dish, cover and cook in the oven for 1 hour.
○ Add the courgettes and remaining tomatoes.and cook for a further 50-60 minutes or until meat is tender.
○ Serve with rice, creamed potato or pasta.   P.H.

Lamb's Liver with Balsamic Vinegar

○ Cook the liver with onions in butter as usual.
○ Just before serving put a splash of balsamic vinegar into the pan to clean out (deglaze) the juices in the pan.
○ Bring to a gentle boil for just one minute and serve over the liver..

                                                                          R.C.

Lamb with Asparagus

4 rack chops	1 teasp. black pepper
2 oz/60 g well seasoned flour	tin asparagus or 2 lb/960 g fresh
2 oz/60 g butter	asparagus, cooked
2 onions, thinly sliced	6 fl oz/175 ml/¾ US cup cream,
1½ pts chicken stock	lightly whipped
1 teasp. salt	juice half lemon

○ Melt the butter and cook the onions until soft, not brown.

○ Coat the chops with the flour, shaking to remove excess.

○ Add to the onions, pushing them aside and on top of the chops so they don't cook further.

○ Brown chops on both side to seal in juices.

○ Add stock.

○ Bring to the boil and reduce heat to barely simmering for 50-60 minutes until meat is tender.

○ Drain asparagus and add to saucepan, saving some tips for decoration.

○ Add salt, pepper, lemon juice and most of cream and cook for 3-4 minutes at which point the sauce should be thick and smooth.

○ Serve in a warmed dish and trickle the remaining cream over and decorate with asparagus tips or chopped parsley.   R.C.

Fried Leftover Lamb with Garlic

1 kg/2 lb cooked lamb, cubed	5 tomatoes, skinned & chopped
Flour for coating	150 ml/¼pt wine/⅔ US cup
4 tablesp. olive oil	(preferably dry white)
3 large onions, finely chopped	salt & black pepper
3 cloves garlic, crushed	olives

○ Dust the lamb pieces with flour. Heat the oil in a frying pan, brown the meat & set aside.

○ Put the onions, garlic and tomatoes in the pan and cook gently to a pulp (10 minutes). Return the meat to the pan and add the wine. A splash of Vermouth or Sherry is a good substitute.

○ Season and heat. Serve with rice or potatoes, garnished with olives. R.C.

DEATH BY CHOCOLATE

Rich Chocolate Fudge Cake

4 oz/120 g dark chocolate,(eg
Bourneville)
10 fl. oz/300ml milk
4 oz/120 g demerara sugar
1 teasp. bread soda
4 oz/120 g butter
4 oz/120 g caster sugar
2 eggs separated

8 oz/240 g plain flour, sieved
Icing:
1½ oz butter
4 oz icing sugar
1 oz cocoa
milk

○ Preheat oven to 180C/350F/Gas 4..

○ Grease two 8-inch sandwich tins or one heart shaped tin and line with greased greaseproof paper..

○ Melt the chocolate in a saucepan with the milk and demerara sugar until dissolved but do not allow it to boil. Remove from the heat, add the bread soda and leave to cool.

○ In a separate bowl, cream the butter with the caster sugar and beat in the egg yolks.

○ Whisk the egg whites until stiff. Add by degrees the chocolate mixture and the flour to the creamed mixture and lastly fold in the egg whites.

○ Turn into the prepared tins and bake in the preheated oven for about 40-45 minutes.

○ Turn out and leave to cool on a wire tray.

Icing: melt the butter in a small pan, stir in the cocoa and cook gently for 1 minute. Remove the pan from the heat , stir in the icing sugar and sufficient milk to give a smooth, thick pouring consistency.

○ Spread some warmed apricot jam over the cake before sandwiching with some of the chocolate icing.

○ Pour the remaining icing over the cake. Leave to set and decorate for occasion.   P.H.

DEATH BY CHOCOLATE

Double Chocolate Muffins

4 oz/120 g plain chocolate, broken into pieces

2 oz/60 g cocoa powder

8 oz/240 g self-raising flour

1 level teasp. baking powder

2 oz/60 g dark brown soft sugar

pinch salt

4 oz/120 g plain chocolate polka dots/buttons

8 fl oz/250 ml milk

4 tablesp./60 ml/¼ cup vegetable oil

1 teasp./ vanilla essence

1 egg

❍ Preheat oven to 220C/425F/Gas 7 Thoroughly grease 12 deep muffin or bun tins. Place a large paper cake case in each.

❍ Put the chocolate into a large bowl and stand over a saucepan of simmering water. Heat gently until the chocolate melts. Remove from the heat and stir in the remaining ingredients. Beat thoroughly together.

❍ Spoon the mixture into the paper cases. Bake in the preheated oven for 15 minutes until well risen and firm to the touch. Serve warm.   P.H.

Alsacien Chocolate Almond Cake

4 oz/110 g dark chocolate (eg Bourneville)

4 tablesp butter

4 oz/110 g sugar

4 eggs, separated

1 tablesp. wholemeal flour

3 oz/85 g ground almonds

pinch salt

❍ Melt the chocolate in a bowl over hot water, or in the microwave on high for 30 seconds, and set aside to cool.

❍ Cream the butter and sugar until light and fluffy, add the chocolate and then the egg yolks, beating after each addition. Stir in the flour and almonds. Whisk the egg whites with the salt until stiff and fold gently into the chocolate mixture without losing too much of the lightness. Pour into a greased and floured 9 inch (22.5 cm) tin and bake in a preheated oven at 170c/325F/Gas 3 for 45 minutes.

❍ Allow to cool for a few minutes in the tin, then turn onto a wire rack.

❍ In summer this is delicious with pureed rasberries, blackcurrants or strawberries.   R.C.

Rich Chocolate and Nut Tart

Serves at least 10.

Pastry: **5 oz/150 g plain flour**
2 oz/30 g caster sugar   **3 oz/90 g butter**
3 oz/90 g ground walnuts,
hazlenuts or pecans

○ Mix all ingredients together.

If the dough is tacky, chill for ten minutes until easy to handle, but do not allow it to harden.

○ Divide into four equal parts.

Draw a 7 inch/16cm circle on four pieces of greaseproof paper and with the heel of the hand press the dough on to each piece to make a circle.

○ Transfer to upturned baking trays and prick all over with a fork.

○ Bake at 180C/350F/Gas 4 for 10 minutes or until lightly browned.

○ Draw the papers on to cooling racks and when cool carefully ease paper away.

○ At this stage the pastry may be stored in an airtight tin for a day or two or in the freezer for a month.

Filling: **2 oz/60 g butter**
6 oz/180 g plain chocolate   **3 fl oz/90 ml/⅜ cup cream**

○ Melt the chocolate and add the cubed butter.

○ Beat in the cream and cool until quite stiff and use to sandwich layers.

Topping: **1 tablesp. water or rum**
4 oz/120 g pain chocolate   **6 oz/180 g whipped cream**

○ Melt chocolate with the water.

○ Cool and add cream. and allow to stiffen. Spread over cake and decorate with nuts.   R.C.

DEATH BY CHOCOLATE

Chocolate Rum Ring.

6 oz/175 g soft margarine
6 oz/175 g caster sugar
3 eggs, size 1
6 oz/175 g self raising flour
2 heaped tablesp. cocoa
3 tablesp. boiling water
rum syrup:
6 oz/175 g sugar
7 tablesp. dark rum

Topping:
½ pint/300 ml cream, chilled
1-2 tablesp. icing sugar

Decoration:
crumbled chocolate flake or
grated chocolate

○ Preheat oven to 350F/180C Gas 4..

○ Blend the cocoa and boiling water together and allow to cool.

○ Place all the cake ingredients together in a bowl, add the cooled cocoa mixture and beat with a wooden spoon until well mixed (2-3 minutes).

○ Turn the mixture into a greased 8-inch ring tin.

○ Bake in the preheated oven for 35-40 minutes on the middle shelf of the oven. When baked turn out on to a wire tray and allow to cool.

Line the tin with foil or clingfilm allowing it to overlap. Wash and dry the ring tin. When the cake has cooled, replace in the clean, dry tin.

○ **Syrup**: dissolve the sugar very slowly in the water and simmer for 5 minutes. Remove from the heat and add the rum. Pour the mixture slowly and evenly over the cake in the tin until cold.

○ Whip the cream and fold in the sugar.

○ Carefully remove the cake from the tin, cover with the whipped cream and sprinkle the crumbled flake or grated chocolate over the cream.

○ Chill before serving.   P.H.

DEATH BY CHOCOLATE

Chocolate Bombe

This is an ideal dessert for a party as it can be made at least a month in advance.

5 fl oz/150 ml/⅔US cup cream, whipped until very stiff with 1 oz/30 g caster sugar
1 oz/30 g butter

6 oz/180g plain chocolate (not cooking choc.)
6 eggs, separated

○ Line a 3 pint or 2 litre/2 quart pudding basin with the whipped cream and sugar. It will stay up the side if whipped thickly enough. Smooth over as evenly as possible, making sure there are no large air bubbles which would turn into craters when frozen.

○ Cover with cling-film and place in the freezer for at least 45 minutes or until cream has hardened.

○ **Mousse:** Melt the chocolate and butter over low heat (microwave for 1 minute on high)

○ Add egg yolks and remove from heat.

○ Beat egg whites until stiff and fold into mixture.

○ Pour into cream-lined bowl and return to freezer.

○ **To serve**: Unmould by placing a warm teatowel around the bowl to allow to melt slightly.

○ Run a knife around the inside of the bowl and allow to flop onto a plate.

○ Pipe some whipped cream around to base and upper rim and finish with grated or pared chocolate.

○ Allow to de-frost in the 'fridge for 45 minutes before serving to allow the mousse to soften.

○ This is delicious served with a rasberry or blackcurrant purée or a tart lemon sauce.

○ It may also have mousses made with chocolate and orange, lemon, purée and brandy, or lighter sorbets. The outside cream casing may also be changed, though this simple mixture is the most reliable.   R.C.

DEATH BY CHOCOLATE

Chocolate Chip Butterscotch Brownies

4 oz/100 g self-raising flour

4 oz/100 g butter

2 oz/50 g caster sugar

3 oz/75 g black treacle

½ teasp. vanilla essence

2 eggs

4 oz/100 g chocolate chips

2 oz/50 g chopped nuts

Topping:

3 oz/75 g butter

4 oz/100 g sieved icing sugar

1 level tablesp. treacle

○ Preheat oven to 375F/190C/Gas mark 5.

○ Melt the butter in a saucepan with the sugar and treacle until the sugar has melted, allow to cool. Pour into a bowl, then add the vanilla essence and eggs and beat for 1 minute.

○ Stir in the flour then fold in the chocolate chips and chopped nuts.

○ Turn the mixture into a well-greased 7 inch square tin.

○ Bake in the preheated oven for 25-30 minutes until firm to the touch. Allow to cool for a few minutes in the tin, then turn out carefully on a wire tray.

○ **Topping:** Cream the butter and icing sugar until soft and light, then beat in the treacle. Cover the top of the cake, then cut into fingers and top with chocolate chips

○ Note : Golden syrup can be used instead of the treacle.

○ These brownies store well for several days before being cut.   P.H.

Chocolate Fudge Sauce

○ Heat **8 fl oz/250 ml/1 US cup double cream** with **3 tablesp. golden syrup, 8 oz/240 g sugar and a pinch of salt.**

○ Stir well until sugar dissolves.

○ Add **4 oz/120 g plain unsweetened chocolate** and simmer.

○ Stir until the sauce thickens, this will take about 20 minutes.

○ Take off the heat and stir in **1 oz/30g butter** and a few drops of **vanilla essence.**

○ Serve hot with ice cream, over profiteroles, on croissants or dip French bread into it for a calorific treat. 						R.C.

Chocolate Almond Clusters

4 oz/125 g raisins

2-3 tablesp. rum

14 oz/400 g plain dark chocolate

5 oz/150 g toasted almonds

1 oz/30 g finely chopped candied lemon peel

○ Put the raisins in a medium sized bowl and spoon the rum over them. Cover and leave to steep overnight.

○ Line a baking sheet with foil or waxed paper. Melt chocolate in a bowl over a pan of simmering water. Cool slightly then add flaked almonds to raisin and rum mixture and with a teaspoon place clusters on a prepared baking sheet. Allow to dry slightly, then refrigerate until firm. 			P.H.

DEATH BY CHOCOLATE

Rich Chocolate Fudge

4 tablesp./50 g butter, softened
2 egg yolks
4 oz/100 g icing sugar, sifted
2 teasp. rum
12 oz/350 g plain dark chocolate

½ cup/125 ml strong black tea, cooled
2 oz/50 g instant drinking chocolate, sifted

This is a good recipe for children to make and give as a gift, prettily wrapped.

○ Line a 7-inch/18cm square tin with foil or waxed paper.
○ In a medium bowl, beat the butter, egg yolks and icing sugar until pale and creamy.
○ Melt the chocolate in a bowl over pan of simmering water.
○ Stir cooled tea and melted chocolate into the butter mixture then pour into the prepared tin. Refrigerate until firm.
○ When firm, cut the fudge into 1-inch/2.5cm squares and dip in chocolate powder..
                                                                                    P.H.

Chocolate Butter Truffles

4 oz/125 g softened unsalted butter
3 oz/75 g icing sugar
4 oz/125 g cocoa
1 oz/25 g instant coffee powder

1 oz/25g ground almonds
few drops almond essence
Coating:
1 oz/25 g cocoa
1 oz/ 25 g icing sugar

○ Beat the butter in a bowl until creamy. Add the icing sugar, cocoa, coffee powder, ground almonds and almond essence and mix to a smooth paste.
○ Use 2 small spoons to shape into walnut-sized balls or cylinder shapes, roll in cocoa or icing sugar until evenly coated.
○ Chill for at least 1 hour. Store in fridge until required.   P.H.

DESSERTS AND CAKES

DESSERTS AND CAKES

Il Tiramisu

14 oz/400 g fresh mascarpone cheese (or 8 oz/250 g cream cheese mixed with ½ pint/300ml double cream, lightly whipped
5 teasp. icing sugar
2 egg yolks
2 egg whites, beaten until stiff
24 sponge biscuits

1 large cup espresso coffee or very strong coffee
2 oz/50 g dark rum
1 oz/25 g brandy
cocoa or grated dark chocolate to finish

○ Beat marscherpone with icing sugar and egg yolks. If using substitutes, beat the cream cheese and double cream until stiff.

○ Add icing sugar and egg yolks and continue beating. fold in the egg whites.

○ Soak the biscuits in a mixture of expresso, dark rum and brandy.

○ Cover the bottom of a shallow rectangular dish with 12 sponge biscuits.

○ Place half the cream mixture on top. Place the remaining 12 biscuits on top of the cream mixture and then place the remaining mixture on top of these.

○ Traditionally the Tiramisu is covered with cocoa powder, but I prefer to use grated dark chocolate which gives a richer flavour.

○ This dessert should be refrigerated for 24 hours before serving aNd may be kept in the fridge for up to four days.

R. C.

Fried Bananas

**4 ripe bananas, sliced length-
wise**
4 teasp. raisins or sultanas
4 tablesp. brown sugar
4 tablesp. unsalted butter

4 tablesp. rum
pinch ground cinnamon
ice-cream
toasted almonds

○ Soak the sultanas or raisins (apricots are good too) in the rum until plump (as little as 30 minutes will make a difference).

○ Melt the butter in the frying pan. If using salted butter skim the foam off the surface to prevent sticking.

○ Add the bananas and cook until just tender (3-4 minutes), turning carefully.

○ Sprinkle with cinnamon then pour over the rum and set alight, spooning the rum over the fruit until the flames have died down.

○ Serve topped with icecream and sprinkled with toasted almonds

R.C.

Stuffed Baked Apples

4 large cooking apples, cored
4 teaspoons sultanas or raisins
2 teaspoons honey/brown sugar

4 dessertsp. water
ground cloves/ginger (optional)

○ Place the sultanas or raisins in the space made from coring the apples.

○ Sprinkle with brown sugar and spice, if used..

○ Drizzle water over apples.

○ Cook on microwave high for 10 minutes, adding a minute at a time if not fully cooked. The apples should end up light and fluffy and almost bursting out of their skins. Allow 30 minutes in conventional oven at 190C/375F/Gas 5.

○ Serve with cream or sweet apricot purée.　　　　　R.C.

DESSERTS AND CAKES

Brandy Snap Baskets

3 oz/75 g golden syrup

2 oz/50 g butter

2 oz/50 g light brown sugar

1 ½ teasp. ground ginger

2 oz/50 g plain flour, sifted

1 teasp. fresh orange juice

4 small oranges for moulding

❍ Warm the syrup and butter in a saucepan over a low heat, stirring until melted.

❍ Add the sugar, ginger, flour and orange juice, mix until smooth, then remove from heat.

❍ Place 4 rounded teaspoons of the mixture on a large well-greased baking sheet, spacing them well apart.

❍ Bake in an oven preheated to 170C/325F/Gas 3 for 8-10 minutes or until golden.

❍ Allow to cool for 30 seconds,then loosen from the baking sheet with a palette knife. Immediately mould each over an orange.

❍ Leave for a few minutes until cold before removing the biscuit 'baskets' from the orange.

❍ Meanwhile continue with four biscuits at a time until mixture is used up.

❍ The baskets will keep in an airtight tin for 1-2 weeks, ready to be filled with whipped cream and fruit and sprinkled with grated chocolate.

❍

For a special occasion flavour the cream with brandy, sherry or a liqueur or chop plain,milk or mint crisp chocolate into the cream.

❍ It is essential to loosen each biscuit 30 seconds after removing from the oven, otherwise they will stick to the baking sheet. .Work quickly moulding the mixture around the oranges as it hardens fast and become impossible to mould.   P.H.

Blackberry Pancakes

1 cup flour	**1 egg, separated**
1 cup blackberries	**4 dessertspoons sugar**
1 cup milk	**2 dessertspoons butter.**

○ Mix together the flour, blackberries, milk, sugar and egg yolk to make a smooth batter.

○ Melt the butter and add to mixture, then whisk the egg white until floppy but not stiff and add gently.

○ Rub a wide frying pan (the ideal pan has little or no sides) with a butter paper and heat until sizzling. Pour a little of the batter quickly and turn down the heat slightly. Allow to brown, then turn over.

○ These pancakes are good if kept small, so don't be too ambitious about making large thin ones, and best eaten immediately.   R.C.

Blackberry Mousse

A simple blackberry mousse can be made by rubbing some stewed **blackberries** through a sieve (remove the rough seeds as you find them) and adding two whisked **egg whites** to every pint of purée sweetened with a little sugar.. Add a little whipped cream, or if you prefer to keep the rich black colour serve the cream separately. Shortbread biscuits are the ideal accompaniment.   R.C.

Apple Crêpes

Apples go well in crêpes and are best if first peeled, sliced and fried in butter and a sprinkling of **sugar**. Fill the crêpes with the slices and eat immediately or roll up and place in a baking dish. Heat in a moderate oven for 8-10 minutes. Flame with **brandy** or Calvados (that superb apple brandy) and top off with **cream**.   R.C.

DESSERTS AND CAKES

Apple Cheese

An old English country recipe dating back to 1843 reminds us of the simplicity and effectiveness of cooking in the old days. It would have been known as a fruit cheese as it was usually moulded and turned out when set. We can just serve it as it comes off the pan or shape it and serve with a rich custard for a special occasion.

○ Pour a **mug of sugar** with **4 dessertspoons water** and the **rind of half a lemon** into a saucepan.

○ Bring to the boil slowly and allow to caramelise a little.

○ When golden brown add about 8 peeled, cored and thinly sliced eating **apples**.

○ Turn down the heat and spoon the sauce over. After about 20 minutes the mixture will start to leave the sides of the saucepan and the apples will be cooked, but will have kept their shape. The sauce will be sticky and delicious.

○ Place in a serving dish or into a mould and allow to set for a few hours. This is a good dish to prepare ahead for convenience.

○ Sprinkle with a little cinnamon before serving.   R.C.

Tropical Crumble

This is an unusual version of the traditional fruit crumble which children love.

4 oranges, peeled and chopped

8 canned apricot halves, chopped

2 large bananas, peeled and sliced

4 oz/100 g pineapple chunks

Topping:

2 oz/50 g plain flour

½ teasp. ground ginger

1 oz/25 g desiccated coconut

1 oz/25 g rolled or porridge oats

○ Preheat the oven to 180C/350F/Gas 4..

○ Topping: sift the flour and ginger into a mixing bowl. Add the oats, coconut and sugar then mix well together.

○ Stir in the melted butter.

○ Put the chopped fruit into a deep oven-proof dish, turning the banana slices in the juice from the oranges to prevent them discolouring.

○ Sprinkle the topping evenly over the fruit and press down gently to level the surface.

○ Bake for about 40 minutes or until the fruit mixture is bubbling up around the edge of the topping.

○ Serve hot with custard, cream or ice cream.

○ Note: Peaches can be substituted for the apricots. Try to use fruit tinned in fruit juice which isn't as sweet as syrup because the topping itself is very sweet. Chopped or sliced rhubarb also goes well with this topping. The porridge oats may be omitted and more coconut added - good for those allergic to gluten.

○ Gluten free flour works well in this recipe.   P.H.

DESSERTS AND CAKES

Upside Down Pear and Ginger Pudding

3 small ripe pears
juice ½ lemon
5 oz/150 g demerara sugar
2 eggs, beaten
6 oz/175 g self raising flour

5 oz/150 g butter
4 oz/100 g caster sugar
1 teasp. ground ginger
pinch salt

○ Peel, halve and core the pears. Sprinkle with lemon juice.

○ Grease a 6"/150 mm cake tin or souffle dish generously with a fifth of the butter and sprinkle the demerara sugar over the base.

○ Place the pear halves on top, rounded sides uppermost.

○ Cream the remaining butter with the caster sugar and gradually beat in the eggs.

○ Sift together the flour, ginger and salt and fold into creamed mixture. Spoon over the pears and level off the top.

○ Bake in an oven preheated to 180C/350C/Gas 4 for about 45 minutes or until well risen and golden brown.

○ Invert on to a warm serving dish and serve with cream.   P.H.

Sugared Fried Bread Squares

Recipes which use leftovers cleverly are invaluable and these Torriijas also known as Picatostes from Spain are superb.

8 thick slices stale bread, crusts removed

3 eggs, beaten

2 tablesp. rum or sherry

oil for frying

2 tablesp. sugar

○ Cut the bread in half lengthways to make strips.

○ Mix the eggs and rum together and pour onto the bread. Soak for about 10 minutes.

○ Heat the oil in a frying pan and fry the bread strips a few at a time until crisp and golden on both sides.

○ Drain on paper towels and sprinkle with sugar. Serve immediately.

R.C..

Hot Peaches, Plums and Apricots

This is an economical way of serving these fruits in a superb countrified pudding from France.

For each person::

○ Cut a **slice of bread** into three and butter on one side.

○ Grease an ovenproof dish and place the bread on it, butter side up.

○ Halve and stone some **peaches, plums or apricots** (tinned may be used) and place them on the bread.

○ Place a little **butter and brown sugar** into each hollow of the fruit.

○ Bake in the oven at 180C/350F/Gas 4 for 30 minutes when the bread will be golden and crisp and the fruit coated with syrup.   R.C.

Date Nut and Carrot Cake

10 oz/300 g plain wholemeal flour

1 tablesp. baking powder

2 teasp ground mixed spice

4 oz/100 g shelled Brazil nuts, chopped

2 oz/50 g pressed dates, chopped

6 oz/175 g Muscovado sugar

4 fl.oz/125 ml sunflower oil

6 fl.oz./175 ml unsweetened apple juice

12 oz/350 g carrots, grated

Extra oil for greasing.

To decorate :

15 whole Brazil nuts

8 whole dates, halved and stoned

clear honey for glazing.

○ Preheat oven to 350F/180C/Gas mark 4..

○ Grease a deep 7 inch/18 cm square cake tin. Line the sides and base with greaseproof paper, then thoroughly grease the lining paper.

○ Put the flour into a large bowl, sift in the baking powder and spice and stir well to mix. Stir in the nuts and dates. Add the sugar, oil and apple juice and beat with a wooden spoon until blended. Stir in the carrots, mixing well.

○ Turn the mixture into the prepared tin and level the surface. Arrange the Brazil nuts and halved dates in rows over the top.

○ Bake in the preheated oven for about 1 ¼ hours or until a warmed fine skewer inserted in the centre of the cake comes out clean.

○ Cool cake for about 15 minutes in the tin, then carefully turn out of tin and peel off the lining paper. place the cake, right way up, on a wire rack and brush top with honey. Leave to cool completely before cutting.

P.H.

Wholemeal Cider Cake

4 oz/120 g butter
4 oz/120 g brown sugar
2 eggs, beaten
8 oz/240 g wholemeal flour

1 teasp. bread soda
12 teasp. nutmeg
8 fl. oz/250 ml./1 cup/dry cider.

○ Preheat the oven to 375F/190C/Gas mark 5

○ Grease a 7-inch cake tin and line the bottom with greaseproof paper.

○ Cream the butter and sugar together until light and fluffy.

○ Add the beaten eggs, gradually.

○ Sift all the dry ingredients and fold into the mixture.

○ Add the cider slowly and beat to a soft dropping consistency. Spoon into the cake tin and bake for 1 - 1 ¼ hours. When cooked the cake should be springy to touch and leave the sides of the tin.

○ Leave this cake for at least 24 hours before serving, spread with butter.

P.H.

Cider Fruit Cake

3 oz/90 g raisins
3 oz/90 g sultanas
2 oz/90 g currants
4 tablesp. cider
6 oz/180 g margarine
6 oz/180 g light soft brown

sugar
4 eggs
8 oz/240 g self-raising flour\
1 teasp.mixed spice

○ Soak the fruit in the cider overnight.

○ Preheat the oven to 350F/180C/Gas mark 4

○ Grease a 2lb loaf tin

○ Cream together the margarine and sugar until light and fluffy. Beat in the eggs one at a time, then gently fold in the flour, followed by the fruit and mixed spice.

○ Pour into the greased loaf tin and bake in the centre of the preheated oven for approx. 70 minutes.

P.H.

DESSERTS AND CAKES

Hot Apple Muffins

These are an excellent addition to children's lunch packs.

8 oz/225 g flour (with plain flour use 3 level teasp. baking powder; with self-raising use 1 level teasp. baking powder)

½ teasp. salt

¼ teasp. cinnamon

¾ teasp. nutmeg

2 beaten eggs

½ pint/275 ml milk

2 tablesp. melted butter

3 oz/75 g caster sugar

2 medium sized apples

To decorate :

1 red eating apple

cinnamon

sugar

○ Preheat oven to 375F/190C/Gas mark 5.

○ Sieve together the flour, baking powder, salt, cinnamon and nutmeg.

○ Combine the beaten eggs, milk and melted butter.

○ Add sugar and pour over the dry ingredients and stir until they are moistened.

○ Peel and chop the apples and stir into the mixture.

○ Fill greased muffin tins (or use muffin paper cases) two thirds full with the batter.

○ Decorate each muffin with two apple slices and dust with a mixture of sugar and cinnamon.

○ Bake in the preheated oven, on a high shelf, for about 25 minutes.

○ Serve hot with butter.

○ Note: you can make ginger muffins by substituting 1 teasp. powdered ginger for the cinnamon and nutmeg. Omit the apples and decorate with pieces of crystallised or well-drained preserved ginger before baking.

○ The apple muffins will not store but the ginger ones will. Reheat gently before serving. P.H.

Bunny Biscuits

3 oz/75 g butter	2 oz/50 g currants
3 oz/75 g caster sugar	2 tablesp. milk
1 egg	2 oz/50 g dark plain chocolate
finely grated rind of 1 orange	(eg Bourneville)
½ teasp. ground mixed spice	1 large packet chocolate buttons

○ Preheat oven to 350F/180C/Gas mark 4..

○ Cream the butter and sugar together until pale and soft, then beat in the egg and orange rind.

○ Sift in the flour and mixed spice, then mix in the currants.

○ Mix well to a pliable dough, knead quickly then roll out on a lightly floured surface to just under ¼ inch thick.

○ Cut out shapes with a bunny cutter, rolling the dough trimmings again in between.

○ Arrange the biscuits on a greased baking tray and bake carefully in the preheated oven for 10 minutes until crisp and nicely coloured. Be careful that the edges are not too brown. Lift off the tray and cool.

○ Melt the chocolate in a small bowl. With a fine paintbrush (I use the pastry brush) brush all the ears, then the paws of the bunny with chocolate. Dab a little on the tails and stick on the buttons.   P.H.

DESSERTS AND CAKES

Coffee Frosted Brownies

3 oz/75 g plain flour
1 ½oz/40 g cocoa powder
4 oz/100 g butter
8 oz/225 g soft brown sugar
1 teasp. vanilla essence
2 eggs

Coffee Frosting :
2 oz/50 g butter
1-2 tablesp. coffee essence
8 oz/225 g sieved icing sugar
1 tablesp. milk
2 oz/50 g walnut halves for decoration

○ Preheat oven to 325F/170C/Gas mark 3

○ Sieve together the flour, cocoa and baking powder.

○ Cream the butter, sugar and vanilla essence until light and fluffy. Beat in the eggs, one at a time, stir in the dry ingredients.

○ Turn the mixture into a greased 7 x 11 inch Swiss roll tin. Bake in the preheated over on the the shelf just above the centre for 25-30 minutes until firm to the touch.

○ Cut into 21 fingers while still warm, remove from the tin and cool on a wire tray.

○ To make the Frosting :

○ Melt the butter in a small saucepan over a gentle heat. Add the coffee essence, bring slowly to the boil, then boil steadily for 2 minutes. Combine quickly with icing sugar, pour in milk then beat until frosting is cold and stiff enough to spread.

○ Cover tops of brownies with frosting then decorate each with half a wal-nut.

○ Note : these brownies are best eaten fresh.   P.H.

Hot Cross Buns

1 lb/450 g strong or plain flour
½ pint/275 ml/1 ¼ US cups milk
½ oz/15 g yeast
1 level teasp. cinnamon
1 level teasp. mixed spice
2 oz/50 g butter
2 oz/50 g dried fruit
1 oz/25 g chopped peel

1 egg

To decorate
2 oz/50 g shortcrust pastry

To glaze
2 oz/50 g sugar
2 tablesp. milk or water.

○ Preheat the oven to 425F/220C/Gas mark 7

○ Put half the sieved flour into a basin.

○ Heat the milk until tepid, whisk on to the yeast, then add to flour and leave in a warm place until the top is covered with little bubbles. This process is called 'sponging' and takes approximately 20 minutes.

○ Sieve remainder of the flour with the spices, rub in the butter, add the fruit and peel then bind with the beaten egg and yeast liquid.

○ Knead until smooth, cover with a warm cloth or put into a polythene bag and leave to 'prove' for approximately 1 - 1 ½ hours until the dough is double its original size.

○ Knead once again, divide into 16 - 18 portions and shape into neat rounds. Put on to warmed greased baking tins, allowing room to rise and spread out.

○ Roll out the pastry and cut into thin strips. Dampen the underside of the pastry strips and use to form a cross on each bun. Alternatively you can mark out a cross with a knife.

○ Allow to 'prove' for 20 minutes then bake in the preheated oven for about 15-20 minutes.

○ When the buns come from the oven, glaze with the sugar and milk/water mixed together.   P.H.

Sugared Almonds

These homemade sweets are a delicious way to finish off a meal, or give as gifts, and will keep for a few weeks in an airtight tin.

1 lb/480 g sugar
8 fl oz/250 ml/1 US cup water

1 lb/480 g whole peeled almonds

○ Place the water and sugar in a saucepan and heat until clear. Add the almonds and stir until the almonds are dry and make a crackling noise.
○ Remove from the heat for a couple of minutes and then return to the heat and stir until the sugar changes to a golden colour and almonds are coated with a sticky toffee and are shiny.
○ Place on a tray and use two forks to separate the almonds.   R.C.

CHRISTMAS COOKING

Traditional Spiced Beef

This is a much requested recipe which is also delicious for ox tongue. The smell of beef spicing in the kitchen is part of the essence of Christmas.

4 lb/2 kg lean silverside or tail-end

8 oz/240 g salt

4 oz/120 g brown sugar

1 teasp. saltpeter (available in a chemist's shop)

2 pints/1¼ litre/ 1¼ quart cold water approx.

1 tablesp. coarsely ground black pepper

1 tablesp. juniper berries, crushed

2 teasp. ground ginger

3 teasp. ground cloves

1 teasp grated nutmeg

2 teasp. ground mace

1 teasp. fresh thyme chopped or ¼ teasp. dried

3 teasp. allspice

2 bay leaves, crushed

1 small onion, finely chopped

½ pint/250 ml/1¼ US cups Guinness

❍ Place the beef in a good-sized saucepan. Add the salt, brown sugar, salt-peter and water..

❍ Bring to the boil and continue to boil for 10 minutes. Allow to cool. Leave the meat in the pickle for 5-6 days in the fridge. Turn it each day.

❍ Remove from the pickle and drain.

❍ In a bowl, mix all the spices well together plus the bay leaves and onion. Rub the mixture into the meat. Return to the fridge for 3-4 days turning and rubbing daily.

❍ To cook : Put the meat in a saucepan and just barely cover with cold water. Place a tight lid on the saucepan and bring to the boil.

❍ Reduce the heat and cook very gently for approximately 3 ½ hours. For the last hour, add the Guinness to the liquid.

❍ When the joint is cooked, allow it to cool in the liquid. Wrap in foil and keep in the fridge until required.

❍ The cooked joint will keep well for about 1 week in the fridge. It also freezes well.   P.H.

Fried Rice

This is the ideal leftovers dish which can use any number of vegetables with or without meat.

○ Cook rice (wholemeal and Basmati are good) according to the instructions on the packet.

○ While the rice is cooking, coat a large frying pan generously with olive or sunflower oil (add a drop or two of sesame oil for an extra nutty flavour). Add a chopped large onion, a chopped carrot or two, a chopped stick or two of celery, a thinly sliced red pepper and turn the heat to low to allow to cook slowly and gently.

○ When the onion is cooked add the frozen peas, finely chopped broccoli or cauliflower and cook for a minute. (Use the stalks of the vegetables and slice them into thin matchsticks.)

○ When the rice is cooked and dry, tip into the frying pan and toss so the rice is coated lightly in oil.

○ Add the chopped turkey and/or ham..

○ Add a generous sprinkling of soy sauce and a handful of peanuts and mix until heated through.

○ Bean sprouts may be added at this stage but are not essential.

○ A poached or fried egg may be placed on top of each portion for extra substance.

○ Serve hot with a salad.

○ Left over fried rice makes an excellent chowder. Add to stock with some fresh vegetables and boil rapidly for 10 minutes.   R.C.

Turkey Stock

Make sure of making the best of the turkey carcass by boiling it with the hard wings and any tough bits of meat.

○ Cover the turkey carcass with water and bring to the boil..

○ Skim off any scum and as much of the oily fat which will rise to the surface.

○ Add a few onions with only the dirty outer skins removed, a carrot, a stick of celery, a bunch of herbs.and boil for a few hours. (You can also microwave it).

○ Allow to cool and skim off the remaining fat before using for soups and sauces or as a simple broth for having with bread.

○ The soup will keep for weeks but make sure it is boiled up every day or two for about ten minutes. It can be refrigerated or frozen.

○ With the stock try making French Onion Soup which is delicious in winter.. Use the good Gruyère cheese available in the shops or fresh Parmesan, though do not hesitate to substitute with simple Cheddar.

○ A simple carrot soup is great with good turkey stock as are mushroom soup, bean and cabbage soup, leek and potato, broccoli, spinach and many of the soups mentioned in the second chapter of this book. R.C

CHRISTMAS COOKING

Mulled Wine

10 fl oz/300ml/1 1/4us cups water
4oz/120g sugar
2 inch/5cm stick cinnamon

2 lemons, thinly sliced
1 bottle inexpensive red wine
1 orange or lemon, thinly sliced to decorate

○ Boil the water, sugar and spices together.
○ Add the lemons, stir and allow to stand for 10 minutes.
○ Add the wine and heat gently, but do not boil.
○ Strain into a warmed bowl and serve decorated with orange or lemon slices.

R.C.

Glühwein

1 pint /600 ml red wine
3 oz/90g brown sugar
2 sticks cinnamon, 2 in./5 cm

1 lemon stuck with cloves
1 wine glass of brandy

○ Put all the ingredients except the brandy in a pan and simmer gently with the lid on for 2-4 minutes.
○ Remove from the heat, add the brandy and strain.
○ Serve at once.

R.C.

Cranberry Sauce

12 oz/360 g fresh cranberries
12 oz/360 g sugar

2 dessertsp. water or orange juice

○ Place all the ingredients in a saucepan, cover and bring slowly to the boil, stirring occasionally to dissolve the sugar..
○ Once the sugar is dissolved, remove the lid and simmer for about 10 minutes or until the berries pop. As the skins burst and release the pectin, they make a distinct popping sound.
○ Pour into sterilised jars immediately and close tightly or cover with clingfilm and use within a few days.

R.C.

Celery & Apple Stuffing for Turkey

1 onion
1-2 cloves garlic
½ cooking apple
1½oz/40g margarine or butter
5oz/150g breadcrumbs
1 tablesp. parsley

1-2 teasp. mixed herbs
½ teasp. coriander or cinnamon
salt & pepper
2 fl oz/60ml/¼ US cup chicken stock
1 small egg, beaten

○ Melt the butter or margarine and fry vegetables and fruit until soft.
○ Add remainder of ingredients.
○ Season well. P.H

Leek and Hazlenut Stuffing

2 oz/60 g butter
8 oz/240 g leeks, trimmed, washed and chopped
6 oz/180 g fresh white breadcrumbs

2 oz/60 g nibbed hazlenuts, toasted
2 oz/60 g shredded suet
3 tablesp. fresh chives, chopped
grated rind 1 lemon
1 small egg, beaten

○ Melt the butter and fry vegetables until soft.
○ Add remainder of ingredients.
○ Season well. P.H

Classic Mince Pies

1 lb/450 g plain flour
pinch salt
8 oz/225 g butter

1 egg yolk, size 3, beaten
caster or icing sugar to dust

○ Sift the flour and salt together, rub in the butter until mixture resembles fine breadcrumbs (you can use a food processor).
○ Stir in the egg yolk and enough cold water to form a firm dough. Wrap and chill for 15 minutes.
○ Roll out pastry to 1/8inch/8mm thickness. Cut out pastry into 24 3inch/7.5 cm rounds and 24 2inch/5cm rounds. Press large rounds into 2 bun trays.
○ Put 2 teaspoons mincemeat into each. Brush side with water and press on smaller rounds and seal.
○ The trays can now be put into the freezer in polythene bags and tipped out of the trays when frozen and stored in rigid containers or you can bake them and then freeze.
○ Brush the pies with beaten egg and cook for about 20 minutes at 375/190C/Gas mark 5. Dust with sugar and serve hot or cold with cream.

P.H.

Almond Mince Pies

Make as classic mince pies but replace 4 oz/125 g plain flour with 4 oz/125g ground almonds and stir 1 teaspoon almond essence into the beaten egg yolk before adding to the flour. Brush pies with beaten egg and scatter 1 oz/25 g flaked almonds over.

P.H.

Traditional Christmas Cake

9 oz/250 g plain flour	12 oz/350 g sultanas
¼ teasp. salt	12 oz/350 g currants
1 teasp. mixed spice	2 oz/50 g candied peel, chopped
8 oz/225 g butter	3 oz/75 g glacé cherries, halved
8 oz/225 g soft brown sugar	2 oz/50 g ground almonds
4 eggs, lightly beaten	2 oz/50 g blanched almonds
1-2 tablesp. black treacle	juice and grated rind 1 orange
12 oz/350 g seedless raisins	2-3 tablesp. rum

○ Preheat oven to 300F/150C Gas 2.

○ Line the base and side of a 8-inch/20cm. round cake tin with a double layer of greaseproof paper, then tie a double band of brown paper 1 inch wider than the depth of the tin around the outside.

○ Sift the flour, salt and spice on to a sheet of greaseproof paper or into a large bowl.

○ In a separate bowl, cream the butter and sugar together until light and fluffy and gradually beat in the eggs.

○ Stir in the treacle, then the flour, dried fruit, peel, cherries, ground and chopped almonds, orange rind and juice. Mix well, then turn the mixture into the prepared tin and bake in a preheated cool oven for 3 hours.

○ Reduce the oven to 275F/140C/Gas 1 and bake for a further 1 - 1 ½ hours, or until a skewer inserted into the cake comes out clean.

○ Cool the cake in the tin for 20 minutes, then turn out on to a wire rack.

○ Remove the paper, turn the cake upside-down, pierce it with a fine skewer and spoon over the rum. When cold, wrap in greaseproof paper and foil, and store.

○ If you prefer a lighter coloured cake, omit the treacle but add two tablespoons of golden syrup or for a slightly darker cake a bar of melted Bourneville chocolate with the golden syrup.   P.H.

Gluten-Free Christmas Cake

8 oz/225 g Bia Nua gluten-free flour

6 oz/175 g soft margarine

6 oz/175 g dark brown sugar

8 oz/225 g currants

6 oz/175 g raisins

6 oz/175 g sultanas

2½ oz/65 g diced mixed peel

2½ oz/65 g chopped almonds

2½ oz/65g cherries

1½ oz/40g ground almonds

4 eggs

¾ teasp. mixed spice

¼ teasp. nutmeg

1½ tablesp. whiskey

grated rind ½ lemon

grated rind ½ orange

○ Preheat the oven to 140C/275F/Gas 1.

○ Grease and line a 19cm/7.5-inch round cake tin.

○ Weigh all the ingredients into a large mixing bowl and beat with a large wooden spoon until well mixed - 4 -6 minutes.

○ Turn the mixture into the prepared tin. Smooth over with the back of a wet spoon.

○ Bake in the preheated oven on the middle shelf, for approximately 3 ½ - 4 hours. Check after 2 hours as ovens vary. Cover with greaseproof paper or foil for the last hour to prevent the top of the cake becoming too brown. Test the cake with a fine skewer to ensure that it is correctly baked.

○ Leave the cake to cool in the tin overnight. Turn out and remove the papers. Wrap in fresh greaseproof paper and foil and store in a cool dry place.   P.H.

CHRISTMAS COOKING

Light Christmas Cake

4 oz/125 g glacé cherries

2 oz/50g glacé pineapple, diced.

8 oz/225 g currants, cleaned

8 oz/225 g sultanas, cleaned

4 oz/125 g chopped mixed peel

4 oz/125 g plain flour, sifted

8 oz/225 g butter/ hard marg.

finely grated rind of 1 lemon

finely grated rind of 1 orange

8 oz/225 g light soft brown sugar

2 oz/50 g ground almonds

4 eggs, beaten

4 oz/125 g self-raising flour, sifted

2 tablesp. lemon juice

3 tablesp. brandy

Tin size : 8 inch/17.5cm round or

7 inch/20cm square

○ Preheat Oven to 325F/160C/Gas mark 3.

○ Wash the cherries if syrupy and dry them well, then quarter them.

○ Mix all the fruit well together with 3 tablespoons of the plain flour.

○ Cream the butter with the lemon and orange rinds, then add the sugar and continue to cream until light and fluffy.

○ Stir in the ground almonds.

○ Beat in the eggs, little by little, and then fold in the remaining plain flour, the self-raising flour, fruit, lemon juice and brandy.

○ Turn into the greased and lined cake tin.

○ Bake in the preheated oven for 2 ½ - 3 hours, covering with a double thickness of greaseproof paper after 2 hours if necessary.

○ Cool in the tin.

○ When cold wrap up in greaseproof paper until ready to put the almond paste on.

○ Note : Instead of glacé pineapple, you can use tinned pineapple, peaches or apricots. Drain them well and pat dry with kitchen paper before chopping and adding to the fruit. Mashed tinned strawberries are equally delicious.

○ Omit the currants, peel and pineapple if you wish and use 1½ lbs sultanas instead for a lovely sultana cake.   P.H.

Plum Pudding

5 oz/150 g fresh breadcrumbs
4 oz/100 g plain flour
4 oz/100 g sultanas
4 oz/100 g seedless raisins
5 oz/150 g currants
4 oz/100 g shredded suet
2 ½oz/65 g chopped mixed peel
2 ½oz /65 glacé cherries
4 oz /100 g brown sugar
pinch grated nutmeg

1 cooking apple peeled, cored & chopped
2 oz/50 g blanched almonds chopped
1 dessertspoon of treacle (optional)
2 large eggs, beaten
7 fl oz /200 ml/ stout or ale
2 fl.oz/50 ml rum

○ Grease a 2 pint/1 ½ litre pudding basin.

○ Thoroughly mix all the ingredients together in a large mixing bowl.

○ Place the mixture in the prepared basin, smooth it down and level off the top. Cover with greased greaseproof paper, pleated to allow for expansion, secure well with fine string, then wrap the basin in tinfoil, folding the edges over well to seal.

○ Steam the pudding steadily for six hours, cool and store in a damp-free place.

○ The pudding will require a further 2 hours steaming on Christmas Day

P.H.

Microwave Christmas Pudding

3 oz/75 g fresh white breadcrumbs
6 oz/175 g plain flour
½ teasp. salt
¼ teasp. nutmeg
¼ teasp. ground cinnamon
6 oz/175 g shredded suet
4 oz/100 g soft brown sugar
4 oz/100 g caster sugar
4 oz/100 g mixed peel
1 oz/25 g glacé cherries
6 oz/175 g currants

4 oz/100 g sultanas
10 oz/300 g raisins
3 oz/75 g chopped almonds
1 small apple, grated
1 small carrot, grated
grated rind and juice 1 orange
grated rind and juice ½ lemon
4 tablesp./60ml brandy
3 large eggs
¼ pint/150ml milk
1 tablesp. black treacle
1 tablesp. gravy browning.

A micro-wave cooks a Christmas pudding in 10 minutes, with the added advantage that the kitchen is not all steamed up. The disadvantage is that does not store well, so it can be prepared a day or two before use and cooked in full on the day. Browning is used to colour the pudding as the colour is not as rich as a one which is cooked for longer.

○ Mix all the dry ingredients, apple and carrot together. Add the juices, brandy, beaten eggs, milk, treacle and gravy browning. Stir well.

○ Turn into two glass or plastic 2 lb pudding basins which have been greased with butter. Cover with microwave clingfilm. Pierce the top.

○ Cook the puddings individually on Full Power for 5 minutes, rest for 3 minutes, then cook on medium power for a further 5 minutes.

○ Stand for 20 minutes and the pudding is now ready to serve.   P.H

INDEX

INDEX

INDEX

INDEX

INDEX

INDEX

INDEX

INDEX

INDEX

NOTES

NOTES